ISAAC NEWTON'S FREEMASONRY

Isaac Newton's FREEMASONRY

— THE ALCHEMY OF — SCIENCE AND MYSTICISM

ALAIN BAUER

Under the authority of the Masonic Institute of France

Translated by Ariel Godwin

Inner Traditions
Rochester, Vermont

Inner Traditions
One Park Street
Rochester, Vermont 05767
www.InnerTraditions.com

Originally published in French under the title *Aux origines de la franc-maçonnerie: Newton et les Newtoniens* by Éditions Dervy, 22 rue Huyghens, 75014 Paris

First U.S. edition published in 2007 by Inner Traditions

Library of Congress Cataloging-in-Publication Data

Bauer, Alain.

[Aux origines de la franc-maçonnerie, Newton et les newtoniens. English]

Isaac Newton's freemasonry : the alchemy of science and mysticism / Alain Bauer ; translated by Ariel Godwin. — 1st U.S. ed.

p. cm.

Includes bibliographical references and index.

ISBN-13: 978-1-59477-172-9 (pbk.)

ISBN-10: 1-59477-172-3 (pbk.)

1. Freemasonry—History. I. Title.

HS395.B2713 2007

366'.1—dc22

2007002967

Printed and bound in the United States by Lake Book Manufacturing

10 9 8 7 6 5 4 3 2 1

Text design and layout by Jon Desautels and Rachel Goldenberg
This book was typeset in Sabon, with Delphin as a display font

For Michel, Sylvia and Njordur, Roger, Marie-France, Odile, Marie-Danièle, Anne-Marie, Gérard, and Roger who made French Freemasonry possible.

For Philippe, and to his finding the way.

For Jean-Charles, who will find it.

For the advisers of the Order, federal advisers, national advisers, deputies and delegates at the convents, Venerables and officers of the lodges who make sacrifices to keep the lodges and the Obediences alive.

For the Brothers and Sisters who live freely in a Freemasonry that emancipates the conscience.

For all those who have allowed me to serve Freemasonry.

For my friends who have shared my path.

For the friend who shared his time and my concerns.

For the absolute freedom of conscience.

CONTENTS

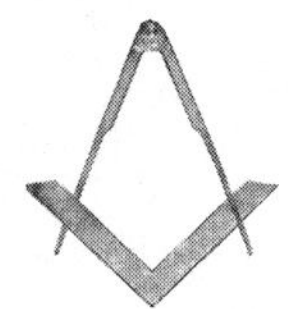

FOREWORD

By Michel Barat, Grand Master of the Grand Lodge of France

History is not an exploration of times past; much more, it is an illumination of what we have done, with the purpose of illuminating who we are. In this sense, there is no history other than the history of the present. This is the spirit in which the reader should approach Alain Bauer's work. Exploring the Newtonian origins of Freemasonry does not simply give us an analysis of the development of the Masonic movement from its origins to the present day; it also allows us to understand the contemporary role of Freemasonry.

This book is as valuable for those who are interested in Freemasonry—either because they are members or for reasons of intellectual curiosity—as for those who simply wish to understand our modern times and our perspective on the future. We all know that Freemasonry is presented as a traditional society. But at the very core of the allegiance held to it, there is a questioning of the nature of this tradition, of its meaning and its development. There is no doubt that Alain Bauer's book will allow the reader to open the way to the pertinent answers. Above all, it is beneficial in refuting that malicious legend stating that Freemasonry is linked to some kind of occultism—when, in fact, its birth was directly linked to the Enlightenment.

The background of the first Freemasons was indeed the Royal Society in England. The desire of these first Freemasons, a fraternity of philosophers and scholars, was for a free exploration enabling man to comprehend nature, the world, and society, to see the things God created by the lights of their own understanding. The whole history of Freemasonry is the history of the connection between their origin in spiritual, intellectual, and moral freedom and the breakaway from faith—which also began in England—in favor of a tradition of progress. It should be remembered that even today, it is in Europe, and particularly in France, that Freemasonry continues to promote this freedom: the freedom of spirit.

Newton's name is certainly eponymous for these times: the philosopher, the scholar who was both physicist and mathematician. However, we must be aware of what the term "philosophy" meant in this era: it meant science, just as much the science of ideas as of nature, everywhere from what we think of today as philosophy to the experimental sciences, the science of nature. As regards the scholastic tradition, the great Masonic myths made reference to the world in which the Temple of Jerusalem was built, and to the great thinkers of Athens. To mark this revolution—this return to the things that made man what he is—modern Freemasonry recaptures the traditions of the builders of those cathedrals which, despite all risks, preserved their references to Solomon and Pythagoras throughout the Middle Ages.

In the image of Newton, the Freemason uses his intellect to build the City of Man with his spirit. In order to do this, he must first pursue rational instruction in the nature of things, in order to open the door to the heaven of ideas, where imagination is no longer a cage but a true creative, in other words poetic, power. Let us not forget that Newton could never have written the laws of gravitation without the discovery of integral calculus, contemporary with his enemy colleague Leibniz. That said, it was a matter of intellect, a capacity for ideas, and not of instrumentalist, limited reasoning. It is this intellect that opens, to use a Masonic expression, "the vast domain of thought and action."

Holding this in one's memory will permit the reader to read the first founding text of Freemasonry—Anderson's Constitutions—while seeing all the connections that the true comprehension of this document illuminates, just as much today as in the past. This text is indisputably a liberal text, as much in the domain of thought and religion as in society. For example, the fact that these Constitutions prohibit political and religious discussions in the lodges is not simple prudence in the face of political and religious power, but above all an affirmation that the lodge does not make religious or political choices for its members: religion and politics are the domain of the freedom of conscience. In conscience, one can be of a different religion from the Prince, but in spite of this freedom of opinion, the freedom of expression remains strictly limited to that which conforms to the Prince. But without this affirmation of freedom of belief or unbelief, without this freedom of opinion, any future battle for the freedom of expression is out of the question. Here one can clearly see how the very idea of progress was established by and in a tradition that is not repetition of the past, but rather a transmission into the future. For a Freemason, tradition is ahead and not behind.

To return to the very origin of Freemasonry doubtlessly means clearing it of some of the distortions of spirit that have sometimes limited or hindered its goal of the emancipation of the human subject, and which have often put a face on it that is not its own. This book demonstrates that every Freemason may state, in his own name, the motto of Enlightenment according to Immanuel Kant: "*Dare to know.*"

It is desirable both for contemporary Freemasons to dare to know their origin at the heart of Enlightenment in England and for all others to understand the great role of Freemasonry in the history of the emancipation of humanity. But this history is also our present. This book can help us to sharpen our intellectual, moral, and spiritual weapons against the contemporary risk of a return to obscurantism. The Grand Master of the Grand Orient of France, in the text of this history, holds firm in a contemporary battle in which all Freemasons must take part: the continual fight for the thoughts and life of man.

INTRODUCTION

Hundreds of works have been written on Freemasonry. What need is there to write a new one—above all, on its origins?

All Freemasons, and most other people, have been exposed over the centuries to a vast inundation of printed matter, most often the work of notorious anti-Masons, presenting them with a strongly romanced history of Freemasonry. In the chapter dedicated to this history, in my *Grand O*, I wrote that this was "a form of street market mythology, revised by some copyists who, proceeding from one error to the next, produced a poor-quality, prefabricated way of thinking more appropriate for a trashy novel than for literature."[1] The charge was severe. Was it justified?

For the Freemasons, transmission is at the heart of membership. Initiation is simultaneously a liberation and an integration into a collective history. Each one is called to take in knowledge, in degrees, bit by bit, of dated references, often referring to the Scriptures, but also to the ancient texts of the craft (the Old Charges). Freemasonry is steeped in tradition. What, then, are these traditions, and what is this history?

To answer these questions, it is necessary to do the work of researcher and historian, to assemble the numerous French, English, and American contributions, to exhume lost texts and fragile hypotheses, to compare, select, and shed light on things. And then to have them validated, verified, rectified, or rejected by others, anonymous or invited to present their opinion in preface or introduction. May they be warmly thanked.

Such is the result of many years of a work that is still incomplete, stumbling upon doubts, hesitating among contradictions. But the reader can be free from the yoke of those peddlers of certitudes who cluttered the Masonic history of the previous century, the continued reprinting of whose works gives the idle impression that it was permitted for them to do no research and the illusion that they knew everything.

Hypotheses, ideas, risks. Here history and fiction are blended, verbatim and mythology. Much more than an arrogant conclusion, this book is nothing more than a contribution opening the paths for further research, for supplements, for possible refutations. The critics are welcome, since they are the ones who allow this to be seen most clearly. Rather than prostrating ourselves before the definitive constructions of the previous century, the time has come to open paths for new research, presenting the historical truth in all its dimensions.

The first Masonry was a masonry of tradesmen working with stone, but also with wood and iron. The lodge was simultaneously the "cabin" at the work site, where the tools were kept, the place of transmission of knowledge of techniques, and the location where the competence of newcomers could be tested, out of sight of indiscreet viewers. This masonry of the work site, the handling of the trowel, is called *operative*, in contrast with the *speculative*, which borrows the symbols of the former but uses only its mode of thought.

Operative Freemasonry was long thought to have been the origin of speculative Freemasonry. People believed there had been a passage from a masonry of tradesmen into a Freemasonry of reflection upon the subjects of society, a transmission or transition between these two masonries. Is it possible that there was nothing but, at best, a simple inveiglement?

Could it finally be revealed that speculative masonry, established in England, was in fact created at the initiative of the friends of Isaac Newton—the known scientist and unknown alchemist—between 1700 and 1717, around a central idea: that science would allow a divided, weakened England to emerge out of civil war? In 1649, England had abolished the monarchy, and then gone through an authoritarian system of Cromwellian dictatorship, a return to the absolute monarchy, and, in 1688, the emergence of a stable constitutional government. The conflict that ravaged the country was not merely a civil war, but also a religious war.

The advent of Freemasonry appears to be linked to this confrontation of simultaneous events, to the influence of the rootless Reformation, the Church of England being the old Catholic Church with a simple change of ensign and the unforeseen secondary effect of the Scriptures being printed in modern language.[2]

For the first time, those who had the means of learning to read and buying books began having doubts when they noticed contradictions between what the clergy taught and what they read themselves. The Act of Supremacy, passed by Henry VIII in 1534, opened the way to an interior conflict that would not be resolved until 1688.

The goal of this English Masonry appears to have been to lead society away from religious debate by replacing it with scientific progress. In short, it affirmed the right to doubt. This was believed to be the driving force of change in society and the end to the religious wars. "Never stupid atheists, nor irreligious libertines," all the members had a reputation as men of honor and integrity—a principle by which no questions needed to be asked about anyone's religion. The subject was therefore entirely taboo in the lodge. On the other hand, everything else could be freely discussed.

Between 1700 and 1717, this masonry approached the question of its existence in a slow process of maturation and elaboration. The first four lodges, which met in four taverns in London, were permitted to do so by the authorities. Their existence seems to have been tolerated by those in power, and in 1717, they decided to unite and created the Grand Lodge of London. Without the creation of this Obedience, speculative masonry would never have existed. Six years later, they obtained a founding text, the famous Constitutions written by James Anderson in 1723. This unified the practices of the lodges in matters of initiation and ritual.

The lodges met less and less in the taverns and more in their own locations, the temples. The newcomer was not let in to the lodge by climbing straight up the side; instead, he was taught to enter the lodge following the "steps" of the apprentice, the route that allowed him to ascend without falling off the scaffolding. The builder's tools, the trowel, level, and square, became symbols charged with meaning. The word *mason* endured. All these things borrowed from operative masonry were furnishings for the speculative lodge—but what was constructed there was never physical.

The codification of the rites also enabled masons to travel, to visit other lodges, and to recognize each other, thanks to the rules imposed. The brothers preferred to rely on secret words, on signs and on touches used for communication among themselves in order to recognize each other and to make known their level of apprentice or brother—although their secrecy, as we have seen, was limited.

Less than ten years after the founding of English Masonry, an anti-Masonic work appeared entitled *Masonry Dissected*, which explained in detail how someone could be identified as a Mason. A long series of booklets and pamphlets, mixing revelations and inventions, were then printed—right up to today. And yet we still do not know much about Freemasonry.

Thus the time has come, on the occasion of the 275th anniversary of the founding of the Order in France, to participate in this necessary effort of questioning and reasoning, to return to our true history, and to reconstruct our memories.

1 A RETURN TO THE ORIGINS

At the opening of the 2001 conference of the journal *Renaissance Traditionnelle*, Jean-Pierre Lassalle recalled that: "Instead of proceeding with a rational study of texts, chronicles, and rituals, the great majority of authors, out of a disastrous desire to idealize Freemasonry, did not describe it truly, nor interpret it, nor explain what they were living, what they had right before their eyes, obsessed by the desire to lead us as far back in time as possible, without any precision whatsoever."[1]

David Stevenson, the Scottish (and non-Mason) reformer of the history of Freemasonry in Britain, asked,

> Why has masonic history been so remarkably neglected by "ordinary" historians? Several answers may be suggested.

> First, one could waste a lifetime reading the sheer nonsense written in past generations by masonic authors, and this has often led academic historians who have ventured into the fringes of the subject to recoil disillusioned, concluding too soon that the whole subject was disreputable. Second, though there have been many excellent masonic historians, their work has tended to be not just by masons but for masons, published by specialists publishers and (though not kept secret) only publicized in masonic circles. A final reason for the gulf that still generally separates masonic from mainstream historians concerns attitudes on both sides. Some masons regard their history as virtually the property of members of the craft, and are unhappy at outsiders working in the field—a response obviously conditioned by the periodic publication of lurid attacks on the craft. Some academic historians, disapproving of freemasonry or suspicious of it, regard it as a disreputable subject best avoided. If historians confined themselves exclusively to studying aspects of the past they positively approved of, our understanding would be limited to say the least.[2]

And it is not uncommon to find confusing (and startling) accounts shamelessly mixing speculative and operative masonry at the hands of authors lost amid synonyms and confusion.*

In 1886, some English brothers had the intuition and courage to found a lodge devoted solely to historical research, insisting on the use of rigorous methods of authentication. Thus was

*A striking example can be found in Benjamin Fabre, "Franciscus, eques a capite galeato," in *La renaissance française*, 1913, reprinted 2002.

born *Quatuor Coronati*, number 2076. Michel Brodsky recalls the speech of Reverend Woodford at the time of the lodge's founding: "In this renaissance of literature and scholarship, of the archaeology and aesthetics of Freemasonry, . . . the legends of the past . . . demand and deserve dedicated studies on the part of Masons who are curious and skilled at scholarship. But when we speak of the legends of the Order, it is perhaps not uninteresting to inquire: '[w]hat are they?'"[3]

With lucidity, *Quatuor Coronati* set about peering into the past, questioning and clarifying the history of Freemasonry, creating the "Authentic School" of Masonic research.

Between myth and legend, history and fiction, adulterated product and revisited reality, there was nothing that was not written or attempted to make believable, because Masonic historiography is generally less a tool of knowledge and more a political weapon. In the face of the churches, their own history, their deliberate alterations of reality, the syncretic contortions required for their implementation, it was necessary to create, invent, and organize a rival history. English Freemasons, and later French ones, excelled at this discipline. Not only did they devise the means of creating the myth, but they often also went so far as to believe it.

We may henceforth, along with Brent Morris, venture the hypothesis that they were also skilled in matters of pure disinformation.[4] For example, the story of the English journal *The Post Boy* (one of the four most important journals of the time, with a circulation of about four thousand copies), no. 5373, December 26, 1723, allows us to see the structure more closely. After the publication of very detailed descriptions of Masonic rituals in the

Flying Post, April 11, 1723, the English Freemasons decided to launch a counterattack. Where force had no chance of succeeding, trickery was used. Taking those elements that had already been published and flooding them with completely false information, they organized the publication of part of the Ritual through an anonymous correspondence. Then, feigning panic and consternation, they managed with very little discretion to buy up almost all the copies of this journal, highly popular because it was distributed by the mail relays. They thus gave the impression that the things revealed in the *Post Boy* were more truthful than those in the *Flying Post*, while entirely discrediting the rogues who used the publication to attempt to invade the lodges. Thus Masonic counterespionage was born in England. (Later, the dignitaries of the Order in England twice modified the setup of the columns of the Temple in order to mislead the curious.)

Interpretation? Reality? It is not truly possible to separate the two, even if Brent Morris's techniques of argument easily draw support: out of forty-two points of reference, twenty-three elements are both precise and consistent with ritual or Masonic tradition, fourteen are accurate but not consistent with the known texts of the time, and only five are inaccurate and inconsistent. But this disregards the essential questions amid points of detail, questions that undergo no interpretation at the hands of true Freemasons.

Be that as it may, the story deserves to be told. It also highlights the various difficulties arising from the prohibition of printing the rituals or of standardizing them. The Masonic Obediences, central federations of lodges, intervened for a long time in the content and form of the rituals, essentially in order to allow visits between lodges at a time when the initiates were identified by means of words or signs. As a result, the bulk of the known texts of the period are given over to operations of anti-Masonic denunciation.

Others made Masonic mythology a veritable profession. Amidst glass trinkets and firewater, diplomas and certificates emerged of arduous rituals and fantastical ranks achieved.

Camille Savoire, Grand Commander of the Grand College of Rites, in a work published in 1924 on the Superior Lodges of the Grand Orient of France, wrote:

> The history of the Masonry known as Scottish, or of the high degrees, like that of symbolic Masonry, has given rise to legends. The authors of these legends are not in the least concerned with historical truth, seeking only to ascribe an ancient origin to the lodges to which they belong, or whose creation they study; thus they link them to initiatory societies whose existence was often dubious, or to chivalric orders in the Middle Ages, without bothering to establish the connection between one and the other. Also, without lingering too long on these legends—whose principal goal was often to create, through mystery, false titles of nobility, in order to serve a combination of things that might include individual interests, self-glorification, or mercantilism—we shall examine the facts. It appears that the superior lodges had their origin among speculative Masons (scholars, literary men, philosophers, archaeologists, mystics, and occultists), who introduced themselves into the masonic milieu around the middle of the eighteenth century in order to organize them-

selves into esoteric circles under the cover of masonic secrecy and ritual forms.

But "classical" historical research also occasionally shows us some surprising things. For example, the most traditionalist Freemasons believe that by decree of the founding texts, women have no place in the lodge. But if tradition is established by the oldest—and therefore most highly valued—texts, then the following lines in the Halliwell (a.k.a. Regius) Manuscript from 1390, the "Bible" of operative Masonry, cannot fail to speak to some consciences:

> *The ninth point we shall him call,*
> *That he be steward of our hall,*
> *If that you be in chamber together,*
> *Each one serve other with mild cheer;*
> *Gentle fellows, you must it know,*
> *For to be stewards all in turn,*
> *Week after week without doubt,*
> *Stewards to be so all in turn about,*
> *Amiably to serve each one other,*
> *As though they were* sister and brother;
> *There shall never one another cost*
> *Free himself to no advantage.*[5]

The appearance in Masonic mythology of the Irishwoman Elizabeth Saint-Leger, the Lady Freemason, merits more than a doubtful shrug. In a notice appearing in 1878, it is revealed that

Mrs. Aldworth, the only daughter of Arthur Saint-Leger, Viscount Doneraile and sister of the Venerable Master of Lodge 44, whose work kept him at the castle, was seized by a consuming curiosity and secretly spied on a meeting.[6] She was discovered, subsequently initiated, and her portrait, clad in Masonic garb, hangs in many Irish lodges. In 1895, the journal of the English research lodge, *Quatuor Coronati*,* confirmed that there had indeed been an "initiation."

In 1925, the research lodge of the Grand Lodge of Ireland also published a study, relating that at her death in 1782, the brothers paid her homage, saluting the "memory of our sister Allworth of New Market."[7] The debate over the initiation of women, or the recognition due to sisters, appears to be less recent than one might think. From this point of view, the founding of the adoptive lodges in France amid the Grand Orient of France in 1774, but much earlier on a local level,† deserves a more sustained attention from researchers and heralds of official truth.

Likewise, could the central myth of Hiram, appearing later, be related to the murder in 1170 of Thomas à Becket, Archbishop of Canterbury, under conditions that were close to ritual? Why murder? It was unnecessary for Freemasonry in the original lodges. It sometimes occurs, even in Freemasonry, that the "master thinkers" turn into "master censors."

---

*W. J. Chetwode Crawley, "Supplementary note on the Lady Freemason," in *Ars Quatuor Coronatorum Proceedings*, March 1, 1895. It is fascinating to read about the almost detective-like investigation led by Edward Conder, published in *AQC*, vol. 8.

†Between 1730 and 1740, by the Mopses. See especially Jean-Pierre Bacot, *Les filles du pasteur Anderson*, Edimaf, 1988.

History can thus be disagreeable for the militants of a cause when they designate themselves defenders of tradition. It is therefore necessary to put in perspective the hypotheses that have emerged, been completed, or been modified in recent years, notably thanks to the courage and tenacity of Anglophone researchers, in addition to French scholars whose works have often remained unrecognized. We must not forget the important work of research on the evolution of names due to phonetic transformation or errors of transcription.

In the course of the same 2001 *Renaissance Traditionnelle* conference, Professor Antoine Faivre, in what appears to be the most elaborate synthesis established on the question of the origins of Freemasonry, referring to the distinction between the history of verifiable events, treated in an empirical manner, and the "meta-historical" approach, that searches for the hidden meaning of things behind the facts, clarifies the difficulty of Masonic research.[8] He tells us that three possible approaches can be distinguished:

1. **The Empirical-Critical Approach**
   Historical analysis is factual and not spiritual. Instead, modern and in full expansion, this approach views Masonic history as an entirely separate branch of social history.

2. **The Mythological-Romantic Approach**
   Based on the highly developed inventiveness of the historical era of the Constitutions of 1723, reinforced by the publications of William Preston,[9] this approach mixes legend and fact, even suggesting extraterrestrial origins for

the Order. All the Masonic literature of the eighteenth and nineteenth centuries was strongly influenced by this approach.

3. **The Universalizing Approach**
   According to Antoine Faivre: "People have sought to unite the symbolic system of Masonry with other systems in order to satisfy a need that is essentially experiential and individual. In other words, masonic symbols are not specific to Masonry, but are rather the expression of universal constants present through the ages beneath various disguises, independent from any question of historical filiation." The connection used most intensively by the adherents to this approach is the link with alchemy. Oswald Wirth was not the least among the partisans of this opinion.

Regarding René Guénon, he is paradoxically used by the supporters of the mythological-romantic branch, and by the universalizing branch.

True enough, as Antoine Faivre reminds us, there are no real borders between the three options, and the crossovers are numerous. In many cases, it is more a question of faith than of reason. In fact, far from being a limited or fundamentalist domain, historical Masonic research requires facing these three approaches head-on in order to attempt to come closer to the Origins.

Between 1390 and 1723, no fewer than a hundred and thirty manuscripts are known of that relate to the habits, customs, rituals, and history of operative Masonry.[10] In 1898, Wilhelm Begemann classified the surviving texts into ten distinct categories (each one comprising one or many documents):

(A) The Regius Manuscript
(B) Cooke (three versions)
(C) Plot (five versions)
(T) Tew (seven versions)
(D) Grand Lodge* (forty-nine versions)
(E) Sloane (twenty-one versions)
(F) Roberts (six versions)
(G) Spencer (six versions)
(H) Various versions (separate texts without a connection to the other categories) (seven versions)
(X) Missing versions (texts cited partially or known in an allusive fashion) (thirteen lists)

The profusion of documents sometimes leads to cross-classification, which is also the case for any manuscript definitively designated as "reconstructed."[11]

From an empirical point of view, most researchers agree in considering that importance must be placed upon the manuscripts of the operatives:

- The Regius (from the Gloucester area, also known as the Halliwell Manuscript), written in the form of a poem, dating from 1390

*The name of its current owner, without which there would be no link to its historical origin.

- The Cooke (from the Oxford area), dating from around 1430
- The Grand Lodge Manuscript (from the York area), from 1583
- The two Schaw Statutes of 1598 and 1599

We must obviously add, just for good measure, the two successive versions of the Constitutions drawn up in 1723 and 1738 by James Anderson.

Even so, it is difficult to trace the existence of a company of operative masons in London before 1536, when the Lord Mayor had to resolve a professional conflict "because their profession had not been defined correctly according to the tradition of their trade, as the others had been."[12] We must go back to 1376 to see the appearance of a delegation of the organization in the Municipal Council of the City of London. In 1472, it became one of the most important organizations in the city. A dissident theory, propounded by Edward Conder and repeated in the *Cahiers de l'Herne* (1992), reminds us that the construction of London's stone bridge in 1176, and then the construction of the new church at Westminster Abbey in 1221, resulted in the presence of numerous masons and required the establishment of a corporate structure.[13]

We then find the Regulations (Masons of London in 1356, Ordinances of York in 1370) establishing the rules for hiring and for respect for local authorities.[14] But in order to establish a solid scientific basis, attention must be paid to the supporting pillars, which are the Regius and Cooke Manuscripts. It is always best to begin by reviewing the elements that allow one to avoid confusion.

Obviously, regulations (modes of organization) must not be confused with rituals.[15] For a long time, the ceremony of admission was not "initiatory." The newcomer was accepted, sometimes very briefly quizzed on the principles or history of the Company, made to take an oath upon the Bible, and told the word permitting him to be paid according to custom. The oldest of these masonic rituals are the Scottish.

The imparting of the Mason's Word was the primitive core of masonic ritual. In the seventeenth century, the Scottish operative masonic lodges took in members who were not men of the trade. These were mainly clients, important personages, and benefactors. The practice of "acceptance" was probably not specific to the Scottish masons, but it was in this nation—Scotland was independent until 1707—that this practice led to a real transformation of the institution. Was this a progressive transformation? It has often been said, but today historians disagree on this point.

In fact, the profile of these "accepted" masons—strangers to the craft—was relatively uniform. They were generally erudite humanists, known for their interest in antiquity, Hermeticism, and the nascent experimental sciences. This influx of important "accepted" masons within a few years suggests an underlying project, but in spite of numerous hypotheses, we will ignore this.

The point is that there is a relatively substantial documentation on the ritual practices of this Scottish Masonry that is the source of speculative Freemasonry. The ceremony appears to be a sort of "hazing," at the end of which the recipient was instructed in the signs and mysterious "Mason's Word," permitting new members to recognize each other. This transmission of the Mason's Word seems to have been at the heart of the ceremony.

Around 1630, a poem alludes to it in two lines:

For we are brethren of the Rosie Crosse;
*We have the Mason Word and second sight.**

Throughout the seventeenth century, there are increasing testimonies from Scotland on the subject of the "Mason's Word." In 1649, at the general assembly of the strictly Calvinist Church of Scotland, many members were concerned as to whether this was a revival of witchcraft, or in any case whether it might displease God. The concern returned in 1652 when it became known that a candidate for the ministry, James Ainslie, knew the secret of the Masons. The case led to numerous debates, and the authorities were consulted. It was finally decided "that to their judgment ther is neither sinne nor scandale in that word because in the purest tymes of this kirke maisons haveing that word have been ministers, that maisons and men haveing that word have been and daylie are elders in our sessions, and many professors haveing that word are daylie admitted to the ordinances."[16]

Finally, in 1691, Pastor Robert Kirk gave the clue: "The Mason-Word, which tho some make a Misterie of it, I will not conceal a little of what I know; it's like a Rabbinical tradition in

*Henry Adamson, "The Muses Threnodie," cited in T. W. Marshall, *History of Perth*, 1849.

a way of comment on Iachin and Boaz the two pillars erected in Solomon's Temple; with an addition of som secret signe delivered from hand to hand, by which they know, and become familiar one with another."[17]

The oldest complete description of a Masonic ritual appears in the manuscript known as the "Archives of Edinburgh," from 1696. Soon afterward, there follow the Chetwode Crawley Manuscript (1700) and the Kevan Manuscript (1720). They appear, according to René Désaguliers, as three enclaves of French Masonry in the eighteenth century. They give a preview of a future scene, and show the emergence of signs of recognition accompanied by an elementary instruction consisting of a few questions and answers regarding the Temple of Solomon and the tools of the lodge.[18]

One must not ignore the semantic difficulties in this historical research. Eric Ward, completing his work of 1955,[19] with his remarkable study of 1978,[20] tells us that the word *freemason,* in the Middle Ages, was simply a contraction of "freestone mason," freestone being a type of very soft stone that is difficult to work with. From *sculptores* to *cementarius*, then *mestre mason*, *masouns*, *fre maceons*, *liberi cementarii*, *fremasons*, *fre masyns*, up to *freemasons*, Eric Ward leads us on an etymological journey from 1212 to 1526, which we cannot summarize here. But he shows in his study, as René Désaguliers did later in eleven reference articles, that the contemporary errors of certain "historians" can be corrected through research on the content of words.[21]

Later, the nonoperative "accepted masons" became the Free-Masons or Free Masons, with or without the hyphen but always in two words, as Roger Dachez made clear in his speech at the third conference of *Renaissance Traditionnelle*.[22]

These newcomers were free in view of the trade, but not unfree in the trade. Part of this confusion was due to copyists in too much of a hurry, and the rest was the fault of careless historians.

The Regius Poem (1390) begins with a prior notice stating that it defines "the constitutions of the art of Geometry according to Euclid." Geometry, invented "in Egypt land" by "the clerk Euclid," then took the name of Masonry. It was brought to England "In time of good King Athelstane's day" in order for "great lords and also ladies, that had many children together, certainly; and had no income to keep them with, to ordain for these children's sake, how they might best lead their life." The king then gathered an assembly of nobles and other citizens to establish a common statute, in fifteen points, and an ordinance requiring "an assembly to be y-holde, every year, wheresoever they would, to amend the defaults, if any were found among the craft within the land."

The lodge is mentioned in the text, as well as the seven liberal arts (grammar, dialectic, rhetoric, music, astronomy, arithmetic, and geometry). The patron saints of the Masons were Severus, Severianus, Carpoforus, and Victorinus (known as the Four Crowned Martyrs), martyred in Rome around the year 300. The end of the poem consists of a manual of good manners, notably at the table. It is composed, according to Edmond Mazet, of a historical account, Charges in fifteen articles and fifteen points, and an appendix borrowed from other texts.[23]

The Cooke Manuscript (1410) is a fairly close repetition of the

Regius. But it appears to be the result of a curious process of placing two different texts end to end, and important differences are outlined by Patrick Négrier:[24]

- The Four Crowned Martyrs are replaced by Cain, Jabal, Jubal (or Tubal), and Naamah (patrons of masons, musicians, blacksmiths, and spinners and weavers).
- The reference to the Tower of Babel is replaced by the two pillars of knowledge, inscribed with the seven liberal arts, which were found by Pythagoras (a new great clerk) and Hermes, the philosopher. Abraham supposedly transmitted the arts of Egypt to Euclid, his student.

Thus, the Cooke Manuscript completes the prehistoric Masonry defined by the Regius. Then the French episode follows (Charles II supposedly having been a Mason before becoming king), and the story moves from Egypt to the construction of the Temple of Solomon and the arrival in England. The Cooke Manuscript also makes reference to its sources, citing several authors and, of course, the Bible.

The Grand Lodge Manuscript (1583) repeats the essentials of the two preceding ones and, among other things, adds Charles Martel to the line of precursory Masons in France, also relating that the first assembly of Masons took place in York. The Charges are presented differently. It tells how "all old Masons or young that had any writings or understandings of the charges or manners of Masons should bring them forth. And some were found in French, some in Greek, some in English, and some in other languages." For the first time, a ceremony of the reception of a Mason is described, consisting of the simple reading of the account followed by the taking of an oath.

The Schaw Statutes (1598 and 1599) appear to relate more to the code of good conduct. But they are at the heart of modern Masonry. Organizing an essential trade in a poor Protestant country, Ireland, the Catholic William Schaw was "General Warden of the Kingdom, Master of the works of the King, and Master in chief of the Masons"—in fact, a mixture between architect and clerk of works, according to George Draffen.[25] According to David Stevenson, the choice of the kings of Scotland to no longer delegate the building of royal edifices to those only temporarily responsible permitted the first "'grit maister of all and sindrie his hines palaceis, biggingis and reparationis, and grit oversear, directour and commandar'"[26] to occupy an essential place in the prehistory of Freemasonry. Appointed to office on December 21, 1583 (he died in April 1602), William Schaw was one of the most faithful servants of the Scottish crown throughout his life. He was also associated with important diplomatic operations, especially in France in 1584–1585, and subsequently with the Danish crown (the wife of King James VI of Scotland was Anne of Denmark).

In 1427, a decision of the Parliament in Edinburgh had given the town councils, and the barons in the countryside, the responsibility of overseeing the trades. Although not much applied in practice, this mechanism was no match for Schaw's reformative will. On December 28, 1598, William Schaw published the first "statutis and ordinanceis to be obseruit be all the maister maissounis within the realme."

The statutes indicate that the Masons should observe the ordinances established by their predecessors, without indicating which ordinances. They indicate above all that an overseer must be elected once a year in each lodge. They outline the conditions for registering apprentices (a maximum of three for each master in his lifetime, contracted for at least seven years, to be inducted into the Order only after at least seven more years).

One might think that the Schaw Statutes organized the profession, and that the old lodges accepted the new texts. In fact, it appears that the texts and the lodges were actually created at the same time. One can even notice the parallel existence of Schaw lodges and companies of tradesmen (sometimes assembling multiple groups, such as carpenters and masons, sometimes composed of the same members). The temporality of these tradesmen met with the territoriality of the Schaw lodges in a geometry of important variations.

The Second Schaw Statutes, dated December 28, 1599, appear to derive from a meeting organized on St. John's Day. They consist of fourteen paragraphs. They define the process of annual election of the "warden within the boundis of Kilwynning." They then define the mode of organization, the lodge, and the responsibility of holding an annual banquet in the lodge. The methods of testing the knowledge of the Craft and of Memory are then defined, with penalties. Next are the dues and the rules for relations with the presbytery councils. Finally, the principles for an entrance examination are defined. The Second Schaw Statutes, a meticulous text that makes compromises with previous customs, allow us to take account of hostile reactions to the publication of the first version.

They even establish a formal order of lodges, Edinburgh being the first lodge, followed by Kilwinning and Sterling. But, as often in Masonry, Kilwinning is second, but the Master Lodge.[27]

In his work frequently cited here, David Stevenson also mentions the Sinclair Charter, published with Schaw's consent by William Sinclair, of Roslyn, in 1600 or 1601. A very short and practical manuscript, the Sinclair Charter is more of a disciplinary orientation, and shows the power of a group defending its territory against the royal pretensions of the Schaw Statutes. The first Sinclair Charter was never ratified by the king of Scotland, and Schaw's death in 1602 prevented the desired unification of trade and hierarchy.

A period of trouble and internal conflict over Schaw's succession began in 1602. The feebleness of the monarchy and interior difficulties intensified the confusion. A second Sinclair Charter, and then the Falkland Statutes, was drawn up but seldom or never enforced. In 1660, under King Charles II, William Moray of Dreghorn was appointed sole master of works, overseer, and director general of buildings. In 1662, Moray left this office to become general warden in Scotland for all trades pertaining to building (including, strangely, artillery). He was forced to resign in 1669, marking the beginning of the decline of this office.

James Anderson, in the first version of his Constitutions (1723), also issued a Masonic prehistory recounting the same elements in a rather remarkable style, beginning with Adam, who "must have had the Liberal Sciences, particularly Geometry, written on his Heart. No doubt Adam taught his Sons Geometry, and the use of it, in the several Arts and Crafts convenient, at least for those early Times." The Tower of Babel is referred to without being explicitly cited, and the exodus to Egypt is emphasized. The Israelites, "at their leaving Egypt, were a whole Kingdom of Masons, well instructed, under the Conduct of their Grand Master Moses, who often marshall'd them into a regular and general Lodge, while in the Wilderness, and gave them wise Charges, Orders."

There are numerous points marking the difference between the editions of 1723 and 1738. In the revision of the 1738 Constitutions, we find the following additions from the 1723 edition:

- A summary of the contents at the beginning, with a division into parts and chapters
- The title: *The New Book of Constitutions*
- The dedication to the Prince of Wales (which is very important in social terms, because the prince had been initiated)
- A reference to the Hebrew chronology established by Ussher, Prideaux, and others, dating the creation of the world to 4004 BC
- The division of the mythological-historic part into chapters
- The death of Hiram is explicitly mentioned thus: "the sudden death of their dear master, Hiram Abif, whom they decently interred"
- The text gives more information on the time of Solomon, and on all of antiquity, including the Roman era and the history of Italy under the Medici
- The chronology of the Saxon kings, starting with Julius Caesar, consists entirely of Masons
- The emergence of Freemasonry in Ireland, up to 1730
- The entire historical part subsequent to 1723

- The list of the Grand Masters, starting with St. Augustine (Austin) of Canterbury

As for the Charges, we find the following differences between the Constitutions of 1723 and 1738:

- Article I obliges Christian masons to respect Christian customs in the Christian lands in which they travel
- Article III refers to the noble, rich, and wise people who wish to enter the lodges
- Article VII covers civil proceedings

There also is a defense of Freemasonry in response to Pritchard.

It should also be noted that in the French translation of 1735 (by Abbot John Moore), entitled *Devoirs enjoints aux Maçons libres*, some revisions had already been made, either by premonition or for reasons of convention. The corrected passage:

> A Mason is obliged by his tenure, to obey the moral Law; and if he rightly understands the art, he will never be a stupid atheist, nor an irreligious libertine. But though in ancient times masons were charged in every country to be of the religion of that country or nation, whatever it was, yet 'tis now thought more expedient only to oblige them to that religion in which all men agree, leaving their particular opinions to themselves; that is, to be good men and true, or men of honor and honesty, by whatever denominations or persuasions they may be distinguished; whereby masonry becomes the Center of Union,

> and the means of conciliating true friendship among persons that must else have remained at a perpetual distance.[28]

According to Patrick Négrier, a touched-up, "improved" version of this translation changed "Christian" to "Catholic" in 1737.

In 1742 a translation by La Tierce proved to be more accurate than the translation of Abbot Moore:

> A free Mason is obliged by his state to conform to the moral code and, if he understands the art well, he will never be either an atheist, nor a libertine without religion. Though in past centuries, the masons were obliged to be of the religion of the country where they lived, for some time, it has been judged more appropriate to require of them only 'the religion in which all Christians agree,' leaving to each one his own particular sentiments.[29]

In the revised version of 1738, James Anderson modified the historical part and took into account the high risk posed by internal divisions over the question of belief in God. But he partly avoided the trap by referring to a new religion, "Noachism," a religion of a universal dimension, predating the Old Testament, revering a Noah transformed into the "Father of all peoples and authoritative for all humanity," whom Patrick Négrier traces back to Genesis.[30] True, James Anderson explains in the Charges that he is referring to the oldest Catholic religion, but is this in a political sense or an etymological one?

But his diplomatic feats aside, James Anderson forced himself to dedicate the second version of his Constitutions to "the freedom of conscience."

In *Ahiman Rezon*, published in 1756, Laurence Dermott defended the traditions in the name of the "ancients," drafting a kind of anti-Andersonism.[31] His critique is particularly ferocious regarding the "historical" part. He relates, in a few lively pages, how he supposedly fell asleep while writing "a History of Masonry for several Years before the Creation," and then, in a dream, was visited by four especially critical friars. Upon waking, Dermott was persuaded not to write any more history, but to draw up the Old Charges instead.

John Hamill notes that James Anderson was often criticized for his "history" of Freemasonry, mixing the operative and the speculative. Hamill defends Anderson, reminding us that the minister never claimed that he was writing "History," but was merely compiling traditions in a kind of "apology." He mentions humorously that in the second version, of 1738, Anderson implicates Christopher Wren for his negligence as Grand Master, thus explaining the birth of the Grand Lodge, as a reaction, in 1717. Wren was not mentioned while still living, in the version of 1723, but was denounced as guilty, once conveniently deceased, in 1738.[32]

In any case, how could one forget that out of the four lodges* that founded the Grand Lodge of London in 1717, only one was founded in 1696?[33] The other lodges were founded after 1700.

*The Goose and Gridiron, an inn by St. Paul's Cathedral; The Crown, an inn on Parker's Alley; The Apple Tree, a tavern in Covent Garden; and The Rummer and Grapes, a tavern in Westminster. See Cécile Revauger, *La querelle des anciens et des modernes*, Edimaf, 1999.

Sure enough, the fact that the Constitutions were published under the auspices of the Grand Lodge must have made them as good as "holy scripture." And just like the Gospels, they remain the primary reference for modern Freemasonry: the Old and New Testament of the Order.[34]

John Yarker, George Oliver, A. E. Waite, William Preston, R. F. Gould, and Alfred Dodd in England; and Paul Naudon, Edouard Plantagenêt, Jules Boucher, and Raoul Berteaux in France have also endeavored to respect the Scriptures without often seeking to find their origins.[35] On the other hand, David Stevenson, John Hamill, Cyril Batham,[36] Colin Dyer,[37] Andrew Durr,[38] Eric Ward, René Guilly, André Doré,[39] André Kervella, André Combes, Charles Porset, and Roger Dachez[40] have all been unceasing in their investigations.

This school of truth—which, in spite of the courage and will of its authors, and in spite of the respect owed to the work of the *Quatuor Coronati* at the heart of the United Grand Lodge of England, and the authors published by *Renaissance Traditionnelle*, has been at great pains to make itself known and recognized outside a limited circle of scholars—has as its basis the process of revelation of a history, of which one can now truly say that truth is more beautiful than fiction.

In his remarkable synthesis of knowledge on this topic (which, for now, concludes our listing of important publications on the subject[41]), Roger Dachez finally establishes a hypothesis known as synthetic.[42]

First, to quote him at length, Dachez summarizes Masonic prehistory thus:

> Operative Masonry in Great Britain developed in a society with limited communication, structured around local powers, in a time when organizations of a national level could have no meaning. In England there were workers, more or less qualified and experienced, and then there were Masters of the work. Some building sites could occupy the entire life of a mason; his Trade would be the construction of a Cathedral, and he would not have seen the first stone placed, nor would he see its completion. It was necessary to pass on knowledge of the building sites, and the oldest, the *Compagnons*, trained the youngest, the apprentices. These men were simple, illiterate, without any surname other than a patronymic. They used lodges, meaning buildings adjoining the edifice under construction in which tools were stored, in which the workers rested and discussed the problems of the site and the projects for the following day.[43]

Plans were also made there, on the level ground that served for making drawings or calibrating measurements.

There was a social and religious order in which the clerics played an essential role. To organize the Masonic people, they drew up texts and regulations, and to give these men a sense of what they were working on, they leafed through the old chronicles, such as Pierre Comestor's *Polychronicon*, to compile a legendary history which would be that of the Masons. To this, in keeping with their pastoral mission, they added Charges—that is, prescriptions of moral character, intended for the discipline of this group of rough men who lived in a dangerous and often violent world.

There were also some customs, some ceremonies of religious character, because this was the nature of all things in the Europe of the Middle Ages: a worker received at a building site vowed to respect God, the Holy Church, his king, and the Master of the site. This was his initiation. This is all we know, because it is very certainly all there is to know. The hypothesis of an unknown network of secret and initiatory lodges whose existence and teachings escaped the view of the historians is entirely unsustainable, at least if one is endeavoring to remain within the realm of history.

Then came the time of the Reformation. The Reformation altered the craft. The sites disappeared and the cathedrals became rare. Other projects had to be found, other employers who would henceforth be called Master. "The Lodge no longer had a reason for existing. This is the reason why the operative lodges have left no trace in England: because they no longer existed."

Even if there were no more lodges at building sites, there were still Masons; thus these companies, or fraternities, emerged, based on mutual aid and solidarity, perhaps even assisting in the search for employment.

The necessary clarification comes to us from Scotland. The benefactors, the nobles or citizens rich enough to provide work, adjusted their charity, becoming "Gentlemen Masons," who obviously did not assist with the work of the lodges, for want of the existence of these lodges. But perhaps, moved by their own political or social convictions, they found ways to meet each other, to gather together, to interact.

This was not a forceful transformation of operative lodges into speculative lodges, but a singular meeting of personalities, all coming from Scotland: Boswell's reception in Edinburgh in 1600, the numerous receptions at Atcheson's Haven between 1672 and 1693 and in Kilwinning starting in 1672, Anderson's lodge at Aberdeen (which, in 1670, counted only ten operatives out of forty-nine members), Ashmole's reception at Warrington, and above all Robert Moray south of the Scottish border.

Only a single lodge was possibly operative in England, and only very provisionally: that of Chester. The structure, called Acceptance, created by the Company of Masons of London, appears to have been unique, with scant documentary evidence and without great influence.[44]

This is not simply a matter of a "Scottish series," but instead a step forward to a reasonable explanation, leaving behind legend for reality. The hypothesis is plotted in an organized framework that requires structure and direction, and must be based on fundamental facts.

Arthur Herman, in his remarkable book *How the Scots Invented the Modern World*, stresses the fact that Scotland, the poorest nation in Europe, was the source of Western modernity.[45] The role of the formidable John Knox, the Savonarola of the Scottish Reformation, in the founding of a Scottish "New Jerusalem" between 1559 and 1572 amid the gradual destruction of the local monarchy, is often underestimated. Knox, an enlightened democrat, defended the "power of the people, for the people."

Knox and his friends, such as George Buchanan—humanist, student at the Sorbonne, tutor of the future king James VI—had a strong influence on Scottish politics. In 1638, the National Covenant was signed, giving the Calvinist Church the ability to impose a constitutional monarchy, and then of establishing schools with a paid headmaster in each parish in 1696. Scotland became the first nation in Europe to impose a system of education for all people. In 1795, out of one and a half million inhabitants, thirty thousand made their living solely from publishing and education. In a few decades, Scotland had produced a highly distinct generation that would strengthen the movement of Enlightenment. Adam Smith, David Hume, William Robertson, Adam Ferguson, John Millar, Francis Hutcheson, and Lord Kames constructed a new philosophy of Liberalism. The Scottish diaspora in America did the rest.

In his *Passion Écossaise*, André Kervella completes the picture, finally going over the history of the Stuarts in exile at the château of Saint-Germain-en-Laye. He brings to light the apparition, emphasized in Edward Corp's preface, of a dissident Hanoverian branch of the Stuarts that accepted Catholics and Protestants and, it seems, precipitated their condemnation by Rome (the bull *In Eminenti*, 1738).[46]

Citing numerous rituals of Scottish "high degrees," Kervella discloses the relationship between Scottish Freemasonry and the Scottish monarchy, centered on the emblematic figure of James VI.

In a ritual from 1763 cited in this book, we find, regarding the rank of "Grand and Perfect Scottish Master," the formula: "Expression of the Masonry preserved in Scotland from the Reign of James VI, King of Great Britain. Today, known to the Grand Lodge of France of the Prince of Clermont under the direction of the Respectable Brother Chaillon de Joinville, Substitute General of the Order and Grand Master of the Grand Elect Perfect Scottish Masters."

André Kervella then relates that at his obsequies in 1625, James VI was referred to as the "Solomon of Great Britain."

Emphasizing the mimetic relationship between France and Scotland, Kervella provides other clues. For example, the nomination in May 1595 of a "Master General of Works of Masonry, Judge and Guard of said trade" in France by King Henry IV, an officially reformed Protestant, cannot be pure coincidence. In his various works, Kervella gives lengthy details, with a great many cited sources, of the other revelations that form a theory specifically developed around these matters.

According to Robert Lomas, always highly controversial in England, Rosslyn Chapel, built in Scotland by William Sinclair, was a replica of Herod's Temple and had the same depiction of an initiation engraved on one of its columns.[47] Although John Hamill, the curator of the museum of the Grand Lodge of England, has long considered this to be nothing but a coincidence, Robert Lomas defends the theory that a line of the Sinclair family was of Templar heritage, and ensured the very structure of what would become Freemasonry. These hypotheses still merit examination.

In a rare 1994 republication of seven manuscripts by the University of Saint-Étienne,[48] we find some elements, often amusing, that complete or complicate the range of approaches, depending on the reader's opinion.

The various versions of Chevalier Ramsay's "Discourse" provide material for this approach. Andrew Michael Ramsay was unquestionably of Scottish birth (1686). A member of the Entresol Club—the precursor of a lodge—formed in 1724 by Abbé Alary, initiated in 1730 into a new Lodge of the Grand Lodge of the

Moderns, a member of the Royal Society, and Grand Orator of the Grand Lodge of France, he is known for his "Discourse" (actually two complementary and progressive texts), delivered in 1736 before the Lodge of Saint Thomas and in 1737 at a general reception of the Order.[49] Ramsay defended a position close to the theses of the first version of Anderson's constitutions in his *Philosophical Principles of Natural and Revealed Religion*, published in Glasgow in 1748,* completing *The Travels of Cyrus*,† published in Paris in 1727.

Here, Ramsay defended a temperate and tolerant monarchy. Cyrus's voyages bring him in contact with philosophers, and he finds God in the Old Testament to be a "pretext for manifesting the superiority of Christianity, starting with himself," as Georges Lamoine writes in his preface to the new edition.

Later, Zoroaster reveals to Cyrus "the secrets of nature . . . to make him observe the marks of an infinite wisdom diffus'd throughout the universe, and thereby to guard his mind against irreligion." He concludes thus: "It is surprising that those who are convinced of the authority of the sacred books, have not made advantage of this system to prove the truth of the Mosaick history concerning the origin of the world, the universal deluge, and the re-peopling of the earth by Noah."[50]

In December 1736, Ramsay constructed a new Masonic prehistory. Drawing on Anderson, Francis Bacon, and the Bible, he

*French edition by Honoré Champion, 2002, with an excellent preface by Georges Lamoine.

†Cyrus, emperor of Persia, who by his decree in the year 536 authorized forty thousand imprisoned Jews to return to Jerusalem to rebuild the Temple.

invented a Grand Lodge in Rome directed by Emperor Augustus, citing Horace (the poet), and returning to Noah, "first Grand Master of the Order." Hiram, "Grand Master of the Lodge of Tyre," becomes the official "first martyr of the order."

After the destruction of the Temple, Emperor Cyrus appointed "Zorobabel grand master of the lodge at Jerusalem." Aside from the aforementioned, Abraham, Moses, King Solomon, and the Patriarchs were the first Grand Masters, according to Ramsay. Following the defeats of the Christian armies, Prince Edward, son of Henry III, brought the masons of the Middle East back to England, then their knowledge was brought to France (by a process entirely inverse to that reported by Anderson, who places Charles Martel on the scene).

The version of 1737, delivered solemnly before the Order and submitted for authorization to Cardinal Fleury, minister of Louis XV, lends a new dimension to the crusaders, "our ancestors." After an expanded repeat of the first discourse, James Stuart of Scotland, "Grand Master of a lodge established at Kilwinning," makes his appearance, going against Ramsay's political opinions.[51]

As one can see, the history of Masonry has been more invented than researched, more manipulated than revealed. Thus it is necessary to find the link elucidating the past, the clue that will untie the knot of genuine tradition, the tool that will free the memory.

The end of the secrets of oral transmission, hastened by the rise of paper in Italy in the twelfth century, and then the printing press around 1450,[52] altered the transmission of the "secrets," as Armand Pouille notes.[53] The encyclopedia, the Reformation, and the Enlightenment were further changes. With knowledge, the investigation of the universe, the rise of the universities, the transmission of knowledge by means of writing, the moment had come for the precursors of Freemasonry to set it in motion.

The Royal Society and Robert Moray probably constituted the elements of construction of this different history of Freemasonry, which ties in, little by little, with Isaac Newton.

2

ROBERT MORAY AND THE ROYAL SOCIETY

Robert Moray, the brother of William Moray and the last true (and contested) General Overseer of Scotland, appears to have been the true link between the revived operative Masonry of Scotland, the Royal Society, and English speculative Freemasonry. David Stevenson, like Roger Dachez, devoted extensive research to him, as do the *Encyclopedia of Freemasonry* and various English and American scholars. But the *Royal Masonic Cyclopedia* has no entry on him in its 1887 edition, revised in 1987. A biography by A. Robertson published in 1922, *The Life of Sir Robert Moray*, makes no mention of his Masonic role.

Completely unknown in France, Robert Moray was one of the sons of Sir Mungo Moray, a landowner from Perthshire. Born in 1607, he was a military engineer and in 1640 became General of Ordnance of the rebel Scottish army fighting against Charles I. After many travels (he also worked for the French army, and was even suspected of being an agent of Richelieu), he returned to Scotland to rejoin the rebellion. As Officer of Engineers, based near the English border in 1641, he was received, on the battlefield, by the Lodge of Edinburgh in keeping with the procedures of the time: a delegation came to recommend him—along with Alexander Hamilton, general of the artillery—to become an accepted Mason. As scientists and specialists in ballistics, they were more likely chosen because of their technical skills than because of their rank.

They each chose a Masonic symbol: a right triangle for Hamilton, a pentacle for Moray.

Knighted in 1643 by the king of England, rejoining the French army in Bavaria where he was captured in the same year, Moray began a long correspondence with Athanasius Kircher, a specialist on Egypt particularly well versed in Hermeticism. He was freed after Scotland paid his ransom in 1645.

He became colonel of the Scottish Guard in France, probably at Saint-Germain-en-Laye. He was a spy and a friend of Richelieu during the same period. He was especially involved in the founding of the Academy in 1635, and would remember this a few years later. For many years, he pursued intense activities aiding Charles I, and then Charles II, against the English. The French, under the authority of Mazarin, still faithful to Richelieu's memory, paid a ransom of sixteen thousand five hundred pounds in 1645 to regain Moray's freedom.[1] Defeated, he returned to France and then to the Low Countries in 1653, and only returned permanently to England in 1660 with the restoration of Charles II.

He was present at his lodge of reception only twice in his life (1641 and 1647), but he appeared as one of those rare accepted Masons who made their membership known regularly, unlike Elias Ashmole. He participated in the work of an operative lodge at Maastricht in 1659.

According to David Stevenson, Moray interpreted the word *fraternity* as meaning a principle of very strong friendship, in the Platonic sense. The son-in-law of Lord Ballacres, the famous collector of alchemical manuscripts, and close to Thomas Vaughan, who published the first translations of Rosicrucian texts (*Fama* and *Confessio*, 1652), Moray was deeply fascinated by symbolic and hermetic knowledge.

His extensive correspondence with Alexander Bruce, Earl of Kincardine, particularly emphasizes his symbolist predisposition.[2] From 1641 on, his signature was decorated with a pentacle.

He returned in 1660 to London, where he directed a laboratory located in the Royal Palace. He participated actively in the project of the history of trades proposed by the Royal Society of London, of which he became the first president. He died in 1673.

It thus appears that Robert Moray was the first Freemason accepted into a lodge and the most articulate on the subject, and that he preceded the reception of Elias Ashmole (1647) by six years, and caused links to form between Scotland and England, between Scotland and France, and between Masonry and the Royal Society.

Robert Moray, if not the first non-mason received (benefactors had been members in London since 1620, but not in a "lodge"), seems to provide the key to the questions surrounding the creation of speculative Freemasonry. David Stevenson writes of him: "Sir Robert Moray cannot be taken to be a typical mid seventeenth-century freemason: the fact that he reveals so much about what masonry meant to him in itself makes him unique."[3]

It is natural, then, for him to have created the Royal Society, along with Elias Ashmole. Ashmole, born in Litchfield in 1617, is emblematic of the "antiquarians" and the connections many of them had with nascent Freemasonry. Besides being a physicist and astrologer and writing important works of historic erudition, he also edited alchemical texts and was a passionate collector. He became the thirty-seventh Fellow of the Royal Society in December 1660.

His collection (despite the fire that destroyed the greater part of his library in 1679) was the origin of the world's first museum, the Ashmolean Museum, which now stands at the heart of Oxford University, also containing part of the Tradescant legacy. Robert Plot, future secretary of the Royal Society, was its first curator.

Elias Ashmole was received, according to his own diary and the documents of the lodge, along with Colonel Mainwaring, into a lodge in Warrington in October 1646.[4] Taking into account what scholars have found, it is highly probable that in Masonry, he saw the survival of an institution preserving the knowledge of ancient times. In an order with a similar purpose, the work he devoted to the Order of the Garter illustrates his disposition of spirit and the nature of his quest.[5] He died in 1692.

Other organizations also prepared the terrain: the Society of Antiquaries[6] and the Invisible College.[7]

In the sixteenth century, some English intellectuals concentrated their interest on the ancient history of Great Britain and gathered all sorts of manuscripts, objects, and accounts on this subject. Between 1530 and 1540, Leland gathered historical pieces from the libraries of monasteries far and wide for King Henry VIII. In 1546, he proposed a book on the archaeology of the kingdom. The next generation continued the quest, with John Dee, Stow, and William Lambarde, whose famous *Perambulation of Kent* was printed in 1570. In the 1590s, with William Cambden, a coterie was formed that appeared as a veritable Society of Antiquities. Cambden published *Britannia* in 1593.

If these authors present themselves as historians, they are not so in today's sense. Behind this collection of historical documents and accounts, there was a project. It consisted of rediscovering, in the distant past of Celtic, Roman, and Saxon England, the vestiges of a golden age in which man lived in a lost harmony between heaven and earth. They all held to the traditional idea that the good of humanity is not in front of us, but behind. It was therefore appropriate to look to the distant past for the lost elements of true wisdom. This desire was also political. The society had the objective of reestablishing the Saxon and Celtic traditions that succeeded the fall of Rome. Sir Robert Cotton and John Selden were its principal leaders.

In Cotton's library, the most important library in the country* and a location for debates, the opponents of the Stuart House who opposed any alliance with the Catholics gathered. These progressives were banned in 1615.

*According to C. J. Wright, of the British Library, "Sir Robert Cotton's library is undoubtedly the most important library of manuscripts ever assembled in England by a private individual."

We cannot forget to mention Theodore Haak's Club, established by this German immigrant who arrived in London in 1625 and died in 1690. He was a Baconian; as Jacques Blamont tells us, he decided in 1645 to start gathering his friends once a week to discuss new discoveries.[8] Among them were John Wilkins, John Wallis, Samuel Foster of Gresham College, and Jonathan Goddard, Cromwell's doctor. Some meetings took place at Gresham College.

For his part, in the same year, 1645, Wilkins formed the Experimental Science Club. Members included Seth Ward, Robert Boyle, Sir William Perry, Matthew Wren, John Walius, Jonathan Goddard, Thomas Willis, Christopher Wren, and Lawrence Rooke.

The blacklisting of Galileo in 1633, a few months after the new attempt to create space for debate and questioning, also indicates the spirit of the times. The prescientific world was dying away slowly, a shudder at a time.

The Invisible College, meeting at Gresham College in London and in Oxford beginning in 1645, brought together the driving principles of Andreae's Rosicrucianism, members including Robert Fludd (the famous Rosicrucian), Elias Ashmole, John Wilkins, Robert Plot, Robert Boyle,* Thomas Vaughan, John Locke, and later Isaac Newton and Christopher Wren. Frances Yates,[9] historian of Hermeticism, wrote about these roots in the 1960s. According to Robert Lomas,[10] this was in fact the predecessor of the Royal Society and Freemasonry; they were formed not in competition with each other, but rather together, in a two-sided, planned,

*Who made reference to it in his correspondence from 1646 to 1647, as did John Wallis.

intentional process, led by Robert Moray. According to Adrian Gilbert,[11] Gresham College—founded in 1597 with the funds of Sir Thomas Gresham, the "King's Merchant" of Antwerp who sealed the alliance between the Hanseatic League and England—was the forerunner of the Royal Society.

In fact, just like the founding of the Académie des Sciences in France in 1666, this was merely the officialization of the creation of previous social structures emerging over the course of the previous thirty years. In Paris, the meetings held by Melchisédec Thévenot enabled Hobbes to meet Descartes.[12] Astronomy was the driving force of scientific research for this whole period. In Tuscany, the Accademia del Cimento (Academy of Experiment) was established in 1651 according to the same principles, under the patronage of Grand Duke Ferdinand II and his brother Leopold, students of Galileo, Viviani, and Torricelli.[13]

This quest for lost knowledge also led to the study of the hidden forces of nature. For this reason they were also the precursors of modern scientists; Newton emerged in their wake, and in that of the adepts of Hermeticism.

The same kind of eclectic interests can be found collected in a personality such as that of Robert Moray, the Scottish antiquarian. There was a strong Masonic presence at the official reestablishment of the Society of Antiquaries, on January 1, 1718, by William Stukeley, who was also one of the most active Freemasons in the new Grand Lodge of London and Westminster.

Some of them had also frequented Saint-Germain-en-Laye. After the defeat of King James II in 1688, his court took refuge in France and received asylum at the château of Saint-Germain-en-Laye. In 1649, Queen Mary had already taken refuge at the same location when King Charles I was executed. André Kervella, in his two books,[14] and Armand Pouille[15] both indicate the strong presence of accepted Masons among the refugees. Kervella writes, "[T]he history of Stuartist Masonry is an immense palimpsest where all the writings are tangled together so thickly that the latest writers can no longer even see the color of the paper." We shall not add to the confusion by trying to pick apart the possible truths, invented possibilities, and distorted imaginings.

In 1666, some of the refugees returned to London. The age of secret societies was over. The moment had come to enter a new era, and the Royal Society would become the crucible necessary for progress.

Founded in 1660 by twelve members of London's Invisible College, the Royal Society of London for Improving Natural Knowledge* marked the development of ideas in England.

THE FOUNDERS[16]

Reverend John Wilkins

President at the first meeting
Born 1614, died 1672
Bishop of Chester
Close to Cromwell
Husband of Cromwell's sister Robina

*It did not get its complete name until 1663. The initial name was simply Royal Society.

Author of *Mathematical and Philosophical Works*, published posthumously in 1708

Viscount William Brouncker

First elected president of the Royal Society

Chosen personally by King Charles II in his Charter of April 22, 1663

Mathematician

Translator of Descartes

Signatory of the Declaration of the Restoration in 1660

Member of Parliament for Westbury

Robert Boyle

Physicist at Oxford

Discovered Boyle's Law of the pressure and volume of gas

Taught at Gresham College

Alexander Bruce, Earl of Kincardine

Scottish

Knighted by Charles I in 1647

Stuartist and refugee at Bremen under Cromwell

Returned to London with Charles II in 1660

Close to Robert Moray

Sir Robert Moray

(see pages 38–40)

Sir Paul Neile

Close to Charles I
Knighted in 1633
Enlightened scholar, specializing in studies on optics
Member of the king's privy council in 1660

Dr. Jonathan Goddard

Physician, doctor at Cambridge
Professor of medicine at Gresham College and at Oxford
Hosted the first meetings of the Royal Society

Dr. William Petty

Inventor of modern statistics
Veteran of the Royal Navy
Refugee during the Civil War at Paris, where he met Hobbes and Descartes
Professor of anatomy, and then of music, at Gresham College
Physician in chief of Cromwell's army in Ireland
Friend of Robert Boyle
Participated in the founding of the Parliamentary High Table Group, along with Wilkins and Ward, which brought together academics, who had taken the place of the royalists at Oxford

William Ball

Amateur scientist, interested in the rings of Saturn
Specialized in experiments with magnetism

Royalist; treasurer of the Royal Society, chosen by King Charles II

Friend of John Wallis

Laurence Rooke

Professor of astronomy, and then of geometry, at Gresham College

Specialized in the study of longitudes

Formerly of Cambridge

Created the first three-dimensional model of the moon, with the aid of Wren

Sir Christopher Wren

Architect

Student of Wilkins at Oxford

Professor of astronomy at Gresham College

Royalist family

Friend of Sir Paul Neile

Abraham Hill

The youngest of the founders (age twenty-five)

Participant in the public conferences of Gresham College

Future treasurer of the Royal Society, after Ball

More a businessman than a scientist

Managed the patents of the inventions of the Royal Society

John Evelyn, who followed all the proceedings, does not appear on this first list. Was he forgotten, or absent? A confidant of the king, he nevertheless had an important role in the constant minutiae of the institution's activities. His signature also bore the pentacle, starting in 1660.

Seth Ward also joined the institution some months later, along with Samuel Pepys. They were joined by Elias Ashmole, John Wilde, William Brereton, and Thomas Povey, a new and surprising mix of royalists and partisans of Parliament. Forty propositions for recruitment were registered at this first meeting. Twenty-four were academics and sixteen were influential political personages. Many of them already knew each other, and some of them had met in exile in France. Most of the candidates were presented either by Wilkins or by Moray. They all became "Fellows" of the Royal Society.

As Michael Hunter writes, "The purpose of the Royal Society was not to teach,"[17] and it claimed to be public and of a national level. It obviously inspired groups formed in foreign lands, as recalled at the inaugural meeting. The Invisible College was brought out into the open. The report allowing its creation was composed by Christopher Wren, professor of astronomy at Gresham College.

Its statutes are very formal and highly detailed. They create a moral personality that surpasses the founders, and proclaims it for the society's duration. Henry Oldenburg, the first secretary, also said that the goal was "to establish their Institution for perpetuity." But above all, also according to Oldenburg, the Royal Society's goal was: "To scrutinize the whole of Nature and to investigate its activities and powers by means of observations and experiments, and then in course of time to hammer out a more solid philosophy, with the widespread approval of civilization."

In his *History of the Royal Society*, published in 1667, Thomas

Sprat, bishop of Rochester, explained that this meant submitting to the examination of the mind all things human and divine, as Florence de Lussy recalls.[18] It is no coincidence that this booklet's cover shows a portrait of Francis Bacon, who died in 1626.

Among the founders were almost equal numbers of physicians, royalists, and parliamentarians.[19] John Evelyn, who was a member of the first council, was the first to suggest the name of the nascent institution.[20]

In 1669, the society had more than two hundred members, chosen according to relatively flexible rules. Men of all religions and all professions were admitted, even while the land was still torn by recurring civil wars. Thomas Sprat, paraphrasing James Anderson a half-century later, wrote: "This is a Religion, which is confirm'd, by the unanimous agreement of all sorts of Worships: and may serve in respect to Christianity, as Solomon's Porch to the Temple."

Robert Moray was its acting founding president from the first meeting, on November 28, 1660, to its "incorporation" on July 15, 1662. He presented the Charter of the Society to Charles II and obtained his approval. Although the king gave it little financing, he granted the society the gilded mace, a symbol of royal and parliamentary power, to precede the entrance of its president.

The Royal Society also acquired rules that belonged to Freemasonry: the presentation of a candidate, the vote, and the regular election (monthly and then annually) of leaders.

Starting in 1662, the society published books, and starting in 1665 a journal, *Philosophical Transactions giving some account of the ingenious in many considerable parts of the world—*

allowing, before the age of encyclopedias, for the diffusion of ideas and discoveries.*

The Royal Society dealt with all subjects: astronomy, light, horticulture, the launching of projectiles, techniques of pistol shooting, anatomy, poisons, cartography, compressed air, and unicorns.†

In order to maintain royal attention and support, the society contributed greatly to the modernization of ships and published a guide for mariners.[21] Members also performed bell-diving experiments (under the direction of Sir Jonas Moore). Marie Boas Hall demonstrates the importance of all this, notably the fundamental nature of experimentation.[22]

Rogers B. Miles studied the fifty-three representatives of the clergy who were Royal Society members between 1663 and 1687.[23] According to Miles, religion in the seventeenth century "was less a reason for studying the sciences than a way of justifying scientific activity." It was a kind of insurance against the intolerance and trials of the past. The Puritans were supposedly interested in the development of agriculture, while the Anglicans were more interested in the physical sciences. In any case, twenty-six of the fifty-three Royal Society members accomplished brilliant scientific studies. They became what Miles chose for the subtitle of his book: *The Clerical Virtuosi of the Royal Society*. Instead of confronting science and religion, the Royal Society allowed a compromise with the purpose, according to Rogers Miles, of "showing that the mysteries were not absurd, but intelligible"—a kind of hermeneutics of knowledge.

*The first publication was Robert Hooke's *Sylva and Micrographia*.

†The passion of the Duke of Buckingham, admitted in June 1661.

In 1663, adopting the second version of its constitutive charter, the Royal Society accepted a privileged link to the Crown and the empire, and formally thanked Sir Robert Moray for his contribution to its founding.[24]

After the Great Fire of 1666, the Royal Society moved to Arundel House, the residence of the dukes of Norfolk. Finally, during Newton's presidency (1710), the society became the owner of its premises at Crane Court. In 1780, the Crown offered a location at Somerset House. The society moved to Burlington House (1857), then to Carlton House (1967), with great means at its disposal.

Starting in 1731, new rules for membership required a letter of candidacy and presentation by two members. This rule was changed in 1847, after which only scientific merit was taken into account.

In his book *The New Jerusalem: Rebuilding London—The Great Fire, Christopher Wren and the Royal Society*, Adrian Gilbert sets the scene, in a controversial fashion, for the reconstruction of London after the ravages of 1666 by a group of members of the Royal Society, supposedly Freemasons, according to a theory centered on the Temple of Solomon. In the 1970s, John Michell took the same approach to the subject of the construction of Glastonbury Abbey in Somerset.[25]

Michell also suggests that the influx of refugees from Bohemia after the defeat of this Protestant state by the Austrian Empire in 1620 accelerated the movement of ideas.

Comenius, in his first encyclopedia, published in 1630 (*Prodromus Pansophiae*), and Samuel Hartlib, in his *Description of the Famous Kingdome of Macaria*, published ten years later, participated in this effort, along with numerous other Rosicrucians, allowing a breath of freedom for scholars despite the political events of the times.

THE FIRST PRESIDENTS OF THE ROYAL SOCIETY

1661	Sir Robert Moray
1662–1677	William, Viscount Brouncker
1677–1680	Sir Joseph Williamson
1680–1682	Sir Christopher Wren
1682–1683	Sir John Hoskins
1683–1684	Sir Cyril Wyche
1684–1686	Samuel Pepys
1686–1689	Lord Vaughan
1689–1690	Thomas, Earl of Pembroke
1690–1695	Sir Robert Southwell
1695–1698	Charles Montagu, Earl of Halifax
1698–1703	Lord Somers
1703–1727	Sir Isaac Newton

If the philosophical link between the Royal Society and the nascent Freemasonry does not seem obvious, then the structural link that will appear later should clarify a reader's questions. It is necessary to examine the position of Newton, the society's president late in life but for a long term, whose influence would be reinforced by an active and determined entourage.

3 NEWTON: SCIENTIST, ALCHEMIST, AND SORCERER

Isaac Newton was fatherless at his birth on December 25, 1642. He was raised by his grandmother in Woolsthorpe, Lincolnshire. During his school years, he was sent regularly to Grantham. He was lodged at an apothecary, where he learned chemistry.[1] When he was fourteen, his mother returned, having married a rich minister who did not like the boy. He was taken out of school and immersed himself in books and hobbies. A hermit with a difficult personality, solitary and secretive, he was admitted in 1661 to Trinity College in Cambridge, at the age of eighteen. With little help from his mother, Newton had to work to pay for his studies and lived meagerly. He made friends with John Wickins and studied the Greek philosophers, Francis Bacon, Galileo, and above all Descartes. At the age of twenty-one he wrote in his notes: "Plato is my friend—Aristotle is my friend—truth is a greater friend."

In 1664, he performed his first academic experiment, buying a prism at the annual Sturbridge fair, on the outskirts of Cambridge. He observed the colors that make up sunlight.

The Great Plague of 1665 forced him to take a long sabbatical (eighteen months). He used this time to improve his talents and develop his experiments with light. He also studied gravity, watching apples fall in a field.

He wrote volumes of notes relating to his studies and investigations, but he waited a long time to publish his research.[2] In 1667, Newton returned to Cambridge, where he was noticed by Isaac Barrow, his professor of mathematics at Trinity College. Barrow, with difficulty, convinced Newton to show the results of his research at a private meeting of academics; among them was the president of the Royal Society. Newton was recruited as assistant master at Trinity College. Later he became Barrow's assistant. In 1669, Barrow recommended Newton as his successor, and at age twenty-six, he became the youngest professor of mathematics the university had ever hired.

Newton then developed a deep but clandestine interest in alchemy, which was intermingled with chemistry at the time. He also studied religion and developed some heretical ideas about the origin of Christ.

In 1671, Barrow showed Newton's telescope to the Royal Society in London, which then included the chemist Robert Boyle and the architect Christopher Wren. Newton was invited to join the association. There he met his rival, Robert Hooke, physician and architect involved in the rebuilding of London after the Great Fire of 1666.

In 1675, King Charles II authorized Newton not to become a minister—as was the tradition at Trinity College—but to continue his scientific studies. At the same time, Newton devoted a large part of his energy to finding the hidden secret messages that he believed existed in the Temple of Solomon and the Book of Ezekiel.

Two years later, during the winter of 1677, a fire destroyed some of his manuscripts and caused his first nervous depression. When his mother died, in 1679, he took a long leave of absence to settle the estate.

The accession of James II to the throne in 1685 led Newton to oppose the return of the Catholics. The deposition of James II in 1688 allowed Newton to rise to an official function. He became a member of Parliament in 1689, but sank into a deep depression and was unable to perform his duties.

Five years later, he became the director of the Royal Mint. He left Cambridge for London. There he also met with his niece Catherine Barton, who served as his housekeeper. He reformed the Mint extensively, becoming its president in 1700 and returning to Parliament between 1701 and 1705.

The astronomer Edmund Halley, having read Newton's unpublished works, persuaded him to publish his more significant research. His *Mathematical Principles of Natural Philosophy* was finally published by the Royal Society in 1687, accelerating the modern scientific revolution.

In 1703 Newton became president of the Royal Society, continuing in this office for more than twenty-five years. In 1704 he finally published his forty years' worth of research on optics, and in 1705 he was knighted.

Newton died in March 1727 and was buried at Westminster Abbey, alongside the kings of England.

These are the details of Newton's public life. But outside his official life, Newton performed "forbidden" research that must be reexamined within the context of his times.

Giordano Bruno was martyred in February 1600, but his writings and research had spread throughout Europe. According to Adrian Gilbert, he foreshadowed Newton's *Mathematical Principles of Natural Philosophy*.[3] Thus, in less than a century, there was a transition from magic to science, from alchemy to chemistry, from forbidden things to experimentation. This continuous process emerged as a natural evolution, marked by Newton's position as the indicator of an essential phase.

The publication in Germany, starting in 1614, of a series of anonymous texts entitled *Fama Fraternitatis, or A Discovery of the Fraternity of the Most Laudable Order of the Rosy Cross*, created the conditions of a veritable "Rosicrucian furor," stirring up conflict between Catholics and Protestants and ushering in "Enlightenment." The alleged author was Johannes Andreae, a Lutheran minister from Würtemberg, who later admitted having written a complementary text (*The Chemical Wedding of Christian Rosenkreutz*). This literature met with considerable success in Europe at the time. Dozens of works inundated Europe, mixing legend with alchemy. In 1677, the release of the *Mutus Liber* (*The*

Silent Book), published at La Rochelle by Pierre Savouret, marked a new era in the complex relationship among Protestantism, alchemy, and esotericism.

The preface by John Dee, the queen's alchemist, to Henry Billingsley's translation of Euclid's works in 1570 also showed the connection between alchemy and mathematics. William Gilbert, president of the Royal College of Physicians, was a mathematician specializing in magnetism.[4]

We must also remember the fundamental role of Francis Bacon in this incestuous relationship between science and Hermeticism.[5] It is suspected that he was the anonymous author of some of William Shakespeare's works and of the first Rosicrucian manifestos. Although a member of Parliament in 1581, a member of the Queen's Counsel in 1596, and Lord Keeper of the Great Seal in 1617, he became the victim of a "political purge" in 1621.

His works, notably *The Advancement of Learning*, published in 1605, defended the right to knowledge against accusations of heresy. But the design of the title page of the 1640 edition is immediately reminiscent of the setup of a Masonic temple.[6] All his other publications, especially *Novum Organon*, published in 1620, confirm this desire to fight against antiquated orthodoxy. His fundamentally alchemical posthumous work, *Sylva Sylvarum*, ends the cycle of his demonstration. It was published at the same time as *The New Atlantis*. There, besides making repeated references to the Temple of Solomon, Bacon proposes the founding of an order of scientists with the purpose of elucidating the mysteries of nature: the Society of Solomon's House.

Newton's concerns were strongly affected by the influence

of the refugees from Bohemia, the slow diffusion of Rosicrucian works, and his own theological doubts. And then there was the affair of the French Prophets at the beginning of the eighteenth century.

Elie Marion, a fervent Catholic from the Cévennes, was stirred by the persecutions of Protestants in 1701. He joined the Camisards a year later. After taking refuge in Geneva in 1704, he came to London in 1706 with a French group delivering prophecies, naturally called the French Prophets.[7] Pacifists but subversives, they disquieted European police forces and higher powers. In December 1707, they were condemned for profanation at a public exposition. They then drew attention to themselves in an outburst of activism, which unusually was successful in that it led to the realization of the events predicted. Because of the trembling of their bodies during their illuminist séances, they were called Shakers. Newton, interested in this movement but discreet due to his new position, is believed—without proof—to have been one of the great intellectuals who paid attention to them.[8]

This strange relationship between Newton and the complex fringes of the Hermeticism of the epoch has long been unknown, and even concealed. The official biographies have mostly kept silent about this side of Newton.

Loup Verlet writes of the conditions of the "miraculous" discovery of Newton's unpublished manuscripts.[9] Put in a stack in 1696 when he was leaving the directorship of the mint in London, they escaped the burning of his personal documents arranged just after his death. They were only discovered two centuries later, and put up at auction in 1936. John Maynard Keynes won the auction, and revealed that Newton was not only the "first physicist" but also the "last magician." The haul included several alchemical works, of which some are hard to access (the bulk of them are at Cambridge, some are at the University of Jerusalem, others in private collections). According to Loup Verlet, Newton's known work comprises 1.4 million words relating to theology; 550,000 on alchemy; 150,000 on monetary affairs; and one million on scientific problems. Verlet considers Newton, from a scientific point of view, to have been a coincidence. If he had not lived, the development of the sciences would surely have been delayed, and the work begun by Galileo and Descartes would have been slowed down. But by hiding away his secrets, Newton the magus also hid the alchemical, hermetic, and esoteric dimensions that elucidated his research. From this point of view, victorious Science made its complex matrix disappear.

Alexandre Koyré writes that Newton senselessly brought his most technical work into the realm of questioning regarding "methodological, epistemological, and metaphysical problems."[10] He explains, in a footnote, that historians often neglect this development, getting mixed up over the various editions of Newton's works, especially his *Optics*.

Bishop Berkeley soon saw the danger, and vigorously attacked Newton's ideas starting in 1710. Leibniz, for his part, accused Newton of philosophical occultism. Newton reacted by publishing his "General Scholium" in a new edition of his *Principia*. He wrote: "The true God is a living, intelligent, and powerful Being; . . . his duration reaches from eternity to eternity; his presence from infinity to infinity; he governs all things."[11]

Was Newton cautious or truly a heretic? In any case, he refuted the purely mechanist positions of Descartes and Leibniz, always remaining at the edge of what was tolerated in religious matters, even attacking his contemporaries for "impiety."[12] Leibniz reacted on the same terrain, writing in 1715 to the Princess of Wales—who was of German origin and would later be queen of England—that "Sir Isaac Newton, and his followers, have also a very odd opinion concerning the work of God.* According to their doctrine, God Almighty wants to wind up his watch from time to time: otherwise it would cease to move. He had not, it seems, sufficient foresight to make it a perpetual motion. Nay, the machine of God's making is so imperfect, according to these gentlemen, that he is obliged to clean it now and then by an extraordinary concourse, and even to mend it, as a clockmaker mends his work." The controversy continued for a long time, mingling theological and scientific arguments in a surprising mixture, often subtle, sometimes of an absolute intellectual perversity.

Isabelle Stengers writes that Newton affirmed: "I do not feign hypotheses, I stick to phenomena." This did not hinder his speculative theories, and placed him in contrast with the "contemplative" Galileo.[13]

In his work on the history of zero, Charles Seife highlights the will of Newton, like Leibniz, to use a "dangerous idea," the idea of zero, to invent differential calculus.[14] Accepting the idea of a number that is nothing and infinite—a strange and terrifying

*Published in *A collection of papers which passed between the late learned M. Leibniz and Dr. Clarke in the years 1715 and 1716 relating to the Principles of Natural Philosophy and Religion*, London, 1717.

concept emerging before the time of Christ, rejected by all the thinkers of the ancient world except for the Babylonians, who invented this empty space, and the Maya, who placed it before 1—the scientists of the eighteenth century used the nothing and gave it substance. Another revolution was in progress: "mystic calculus" appeared.

In 1669, according to Richard Westfall, Newton immersed himself in alchemical literature.[15] Betty Jo Teeter Dobbs affirms that "Newton read virtually everything alchemical that had ever been published, and a good many things that had not."[16] Numerous manuscripts from Hartlib's circle were copied by Newton himself. His friend Robert Boyle served him as a link to other circles of Rosicrucians and alchemists. Elias Ashmole did the same in writing his *Theatrum Chemicum Britannicum* (published in 1652).

Newton even devised an anagram of his name as a pseudonym (*Isaacus Neuutonus* becoming *Jeova sanctus unus*), which allowed him to exchange manuscripts with his correspondents while remaining anonymous, despite widespread speculation. In Newton's personal archives, a great many manuscripts have been found with lengthy annotations: Philalethes' *Secrets Reveal'd* from 1669, Sendivogius's *Novum Lumen Chymicum*, Espagnet's *Arcanum hermeticae philosophiae*, Maier's *Symbola aureae mensae duodecim*, the *Opera* of George Ripley (the great English alchemist), and Basil Valentine's *Triumphal Chariot of Antimony*. Most of these are preserved at the Hebrew University of Jerusalem.

Newton was fascinated by the transmutation of metals. "Far from seeking to make gold, he attempted to understand nature," writes Jacques Blamont. Newton attempted to isolate mercury, a fundamental element. This was probably the cause of his death.

Outside this dimension, Newton developed truly heretical ideas. Fascinated by the trinity, he was impassioned by the conflict between the orthodox, led by Athanasius in the fourth century, and the disciples of Arius. Arius believed that God was one, and that the trinity could not be. Newton, according to Richard Westfall, became convinced bit by bit "that a massive fraud had perverted the legacy of the early church."[17] Newton considered the worship of Christ, in place of God, to be idolatrous. But Newton, in a completely orthodox Cambridge where his own master, Barrow, defended the trinity, did not express his views publicly.

David Brewster, in his 1855 biography, wrote, "[U]niting philosophy and religion, he dissolved the alliance that genius had formed with skepticism, and added to the myriad witnesses the most brilliant name of ancient and modern times."[18]

Isabelle Stengers, exhuming the evidence gathered by John Conduitt, the husband of one of Newton's nieces, writes of Newton's staying up to all hours with his chemical and alchemical projects.[19] This is echoed by Humphrey Newton (not related to Isaac), his laboratory assistant from 1685 to 1690, as well as William Stukeley and David Brewster. Brewster expresses his incomprehension of this fascination common to Newton, Locke, and Boyle.[20]

For her part, Margaret C. Jacob emphasizes Newton's role in the restoration of a social interpretation of philosophy and the sciences during a time when the Latitudinarians were trying to assert themselves from all directions.

In 1968, Franck Manuel loudly broke the embarrassed silence and revealed the hidden face of the great man.[21] Richard Westfall completed the work, affirming the "interpenetration" of the two sides of Newton, especially in his work on enlightenment.

According to Isabelle Stengers, this was the most extensive affirmation, bringing forward the fact that "Newton's alchemy was not an embarrassing fault that he had to hide, but an essential source of inspiration without which the dismal ontology of the mechanists would have threatened to suffocate him with empty mechanical analogies." The controversy continued afterward. Betty Jo Teeter Dobbs[22] confirms, along with Paolo Rossi:

> A recognition of the troubled waters at the origin of modern science, an awareness that the birth of scientific learning is not quite as aseptic as the men of the Enlightenment and the positivists naively assumed, does not imply either a denial of the existence of scientific knowledge, or a surrender to primitivism and cult of magic. Must disillusionment necessarily coincide with a desire for regression?[23]

A. Rupert Hall, in another biography that expands theses put forward in various works since 1963[24] (Hall also supervised the publication of the letters of Henry Oldenburg, the secretary of the Royal Society), admits this uniqueness: "Newton was the last polymath, the last mind to believe that all knowledge was within its grasp." I. Bernard Cohen denies this firmly in two of his works, and remains impassive on this subject.[25]

Betty Jo Teeter Dobbs performed the most complete synthesis

of the current research, stating that Newton was successful, having the crucial freedom to move forward in his search for the truth:

> Newton wished to penetrate to the divine principles beyond the veil of nature, and beyond the veils of human record and received revelation as well. His goal was the knowledge of God, and for achieving that goal he marshaled the evidence from every source available to him: mathematics, experiment, observation, reason, revelation, historical record, myth, the tattered remnants of ancient wisdom.

Newton was not a skeptic:

> Not only did Newton respect the idea that Truth was accessible to the human mind, but also he was very much inclined to accord to several systems of thought the right to claim access to some aspect of the Truth.[26]

And to quote Newton's translation of the *Emerald Tablet* of Hermes Trismegistus, from between 1680 and 1684:

> By this means you shall have the glory of the whole world and thereby all obscurity shall fly from you.[27]

We can no longer ignore the connection, emphasized by Margaret C. Jacob, to the "Free Thinkers" and the contention that existed between them and the first Freemasons. John Tolland's position in this controversy alone merits a long exposition.

Newton's influence on the works of Adam Smith, the Scottish economist, should also not remain ignored by scholars.

According to Loup Verlet, the fact that Newton was born on December 25 might have made him believe that he would be a new Messiah, another Christ. According to Nicholas Fatio de Duillier, Newton found that one anagram of "Isaacus Newtonus" was "ieova sanctus unus."* He even attempted to prove that the date of the birth of Christ had been falsified. Was this the sin of pride?

It is true that Newton was fascinated by the end of time, and he believed the great comet of 1680 to be an omen. In any case, from either prudence or anxiety, Newton did not try to calculate the moment of the apocalypse. His emotional relationships, his fatigue, and the secondary effects of his experiments—notably with antimony—could also have been reasons for this research.

Was Newton influenced by the forbidden or did he succeed in using the best of it to build a space of freedom in which a well-controlled science could finally give birth to progress? Was this the link between the realm of spirituality and the vitality of the conscience?

According to David Stevenson, a probable source for the drafting of the Charges was the printing by James Anderson of the texts compiled by his father, the longtime secretary of the Lodge of Aberdeen.† The time had come for Freemasonry to emerge: the incestuous child of research, theology, and freedom.

*See Nicolas Witkowski, *Une histoire sentimentale des sciences*, Seuil, March 2003.

†See the complete article: "James Anderson, Man and Mason," in *Heredom*, vol. 10, 2002.

4

THE BIRTH OF FREEMASONRY

Steven L. Kaplan explains at length the collapse of the social structures of the old French monarchy. In the eighteenth century, there were hundreds of trades and thousands of corporations.[1] (At the demand of Louis IX, the book of trades compiled by Étienne Boileau, the provost of Paris, established regulations for about a hundred of them.) There were some forty thousand "masters" and around a hundred thousand laborers. Between 1776 and 1791, this force of social resistance to economic modernization resisted Turgot, bowed before the d'Allarde Law, and gave in to the Le Chapelier Law in the name of the revolution that was in progress. Nothing was said regarding the place and role of Freemasonry. Only in England were there still corporations and guilds. As for the connection with operative Masonry, David Stevenson's work is sufficient to settle the question of the English side.

In her chapter concisely entitled "Maçonnerie," Margaret C. Jacob returns to the theory of transition, citing the founding of a "libertine and masonic group" in 1710 in The Hague.[2] They called themselves Brothers, had a Grand Master and a Secretary, and were composed of Huguenot intellectuals from France. Jacob, in her main works, develops further theories on the relationship between the founding of a new civil society and the role of English Freemasonry. In *Living the Enlightenment*,[3] *The Radical Enlightenment*,[4] and especially *The Newtonians and the English Revolution*,[5] she explores the connections among the English Revolution, the ideas of Hermeticism, philosophical oppositions, scientific clubs, and the role of Freemasonry.

Without stating a definite position, Jacob notes the political vision and ideological content of speculative Freemasonry in England. In a long discussion on "Newtonian Enlightenment and its critics," she points out the link between Newton's research and its popularization in France by Voltaire, then its return in a translated version to England.

Jérôme Rousse-Lacordaire also insists on "the ambivalence of Enlightenment."[6] He describes the point at which the philosophy of the Royal Society was infused into scientific and erudite society, according to Thomas Sprat, the official historian of the Royal Society, in 1677:

> As for what belongs to the Members themselves, that are to constitute the Society: It is to be noted, that they have freely admitted Men of different Religions, Countries, and

> Professions of Life. This they were oblig'd to do, or else they would come far short of the largeness of their own Declarations. For they openly profess, not to lay the Foundation of an English, Scotch, Irish, Popish, or Protestant Philosophy; but of a Philosophy of Mankind.[7]

Scientific experimentation, questioning, and research were all part of the stated desires of the Royal Society, as well as in the syncretism clandestinely exercised by Newton.

In essence, Freemasonry appears to be a *sui generis* expression. Was Isaac Newton the initiator, the founder, or the accomplice?

Quoting the dedication preceding a poem published after Newton's death by John Theophilus Desaguliers (1683–1744), disciple and secretary of Newton, Fellow of the Royal Society starting in 1714, and chaplain to the Prince of Wales, Rousse-Lacordaire establishes the connection between Newton's philosophy and politics:[8]

> Here he explains in effect that the "Laws of Nations" must be analogous to the "Laws of Nature which are establish'd in the Heavens" and that they can be studied "as a Phænomenon." As this study permitted him, he "look'd upon that Form of [government] to be most perfect, which did most nearly resemble the Natural Government of our System, according to the Laws settled by the All-Wise and Almighty Architect of the Universe."*

*Jérôme Rousse-Lacordaire: "Les Lumières Maçonniques entre naturalisme et illuminisme," in *Discursos e Práticas Alquímicas*, vol. 2, Lisbon: Hugin Editores, 2003.

After his election as the curator of experimentation for the Royal Society, Desaguliers appeared as the *deus ex machina* of the creation of speculative Freemasonry. If Freemasonry were a religion, Newton would be Christ the Messiah and Desaguliers his prophet.

Right from the start, Desaguliers' life was a testimony to all the religious strife and intellectual debates of late-seventeenth-century Europe. He expressed values that were naturally found in the sources of English speculative Masonry in London in the 1720s.

The son of a minister from La Rochelle, forced into exile by the revocation of the Edict of Nantes in 1685, the young Desaguliers, hidden in a barrel, fled France with his parents in order to escape the law requiring exiled Protestants to leave their children in France to be raised as Catholics. Is it any surprise that later, once renowned and influential, he showed an open hostility to the memory of Louis XIV and his despotism? Such childhood memories would have to remain stronger than any political reasoning.

Noticed very early on for his abilities and gifts, he went to the prestigious Christ Church College, Oxford. Although the course of studies still followed the classical pattern, special attention was already being paid to the philosophy of Locke, who was also a former student at Christ Church. In the realm of scientific knowledge, Locke was especially opposed to the innatism of the Neoplatonists at Cambridge—for whom all truth came from a divine predisposition—and, in the domains of politics and religion, to defining and justifying the concept of tolerance.

Known for his talents as an experimenter since 1710, Desaguliers approached the Royal Society in 1713 and was elected to it a year later, under the prestigious patronage of its president, Newton himself. Thus Desaguliers began a brilliant career, following closely in the wake of the inaccessible great man. According to one of his best biographers, "It is possible that, being elected Fellow of the Royal Society three years after the death of Queen Anne, Desaguliers may also have seen himself as being entrusted with the mission of reaffirming Newtonian supremacy in matters of natural philosophy."[9] He would work at this task until the end of his days.

Admitted to the diaconate in 1710, then ordained a priest in December 1717, Reverend Desaguliers, except in the honorary function of chaplain to high aristocrats and a few ecclesiastical charities, left behind only two sermons, which were obviously not his most brilliant literary efforts. In contrast, earning his doctorate in 1718, the course of his life was profoundly affected by this degree in law, which was the completion of his university studies.

Regarding the immense amount of work done by Desaguliers over more than thirty years of experimentation, reflection, lectures, and publications, we can agree with Pierre Boutin:

> The entirety of Desaguliers' work is in keeping with the context of the philosophical thought of seventeenth-century England. This thought is particularly marked by an evolution of principles and methodologies in matters of natural philosophy. The study of the phenomena of nature is considered as already set apart from the search for knowledge of God, in the sense that physical reality is not provided by the divine word; nor is it authenticated by the testimony of Scripture;

> the results of experimentation, which make it comprehensible, can be grasped by reading geometric figures. The physical functioning of the universe then becomes intelligible to the human mind. Besides bringing about an analytical reflection upon the foundations of faith, this new concept of truth makes one imagine new relations between man and the government of all things.[10]

In this context, we disregard what led Desaguliers to the lodges, and do not even know where or when he was initiated! However, as Grand Master of the Grand Lodge of London (the Moderns) from 1719 on, Desaguliers succeeded, according to Roger Dachez, in "conquering" the brand new Grand Lodge. Taking over from a modest unknown man, Anthony Sayer, he passed on the office of Grand Master in 1721 to the Duke of Montague, the richest man in England and also a medical doctor. Together, the Hanoverian nobility and the scientists of the Royal Society formed the new British aristocracy. The First Grand Lodge, the seedling of the nation's Freemasonry, was truly born. A liberal intellectual and political elite was working for peace in Great Britain, offering as a pledge the creation of highly powerful charitable works: the first charitable committee had been formed. Sayer, forgotten and penniless, appealed to it.

In his 1967 study, J. R. Clarke points out that James Anderson, in his preface to the first constitutions, wrote that "several Noblemen and Gentlemen of the best Rank, with Clergymen and learned Scholars," had joined the Order under the presidency of the Duke of Montague.[11] The *AQC* has made numerous attempts to establish a connection between the Royal Society and the founding of the Grand Lodge of London, without much success. J. R. Clarke then endeavored to find connections in the lists of members, despite the risk of error.

In 1723, out of two hundred members of the Royal Society, about forty were also Freemasons, making up a fifth of the total. But more importantly, thirteen members belonged to the Royal Society before the foundation of the Grand Lodge, and a considerable portion of these members were Grand Masters. In 1725, forty-seven Fellows belonged to the Grand Lodge. (There were sixty-four Lodges with a membership of two hundred Brothers.[12])

The Grand Masters of the Grand Lodge of London and the Royal Society		
Name	Grand Master in:	Member of the Royal Society in:
John Theophilus Desaguliers	1719	1714
Duke of Montague	1721	1718
Duke of Buccleuch	1723	1724
Duke of Richmond	1724	1724
Earl of Abercorn	1725	1715
Lord Coleraine	1727	1735
Earl of Leicester	1731	1729
Earl of Strathmore	1733	1732

Grand Masters (continued)		
Name	Grand Master in:	Member of the Royal Society in:
Earl of Crawford	1734	1732
Earl of Loudon	1736	1738
Earl Darnley	1737	1738
Lord Raymond	1739	1740
Earl of Morton	1741	1733
Earl of Morton	1757	1754
Earl Ferrers	1762	1761
Lord Petre	1772	1780
Duke of Cumberland	1782	1789
Prince of Wales	1790	1820
Lord Moira (Deputy Grand Master)	1790	1787
Duke of Sussex	1813	1828
Assistant Grand Masters		
John Beale	1721	1721
Martin Folkes	1724	1714
William Graeme	1739	1730
Martin Clare	1741	1735
Edward Hody	1745	1733
Viscount Dillon	1768	1767

Some Grand Masters were also members of Gresham College, the Invisible College, or the Society of Antiquaries (e.g., John Machin and Philip Carteret Webb).

In addition to the other directors of the Grand Lodge of London, we also find twenty-three Grand Overseers who were members of the Royal Society between 1723 and 1813. This was along the same principles as the Grand Lodge of London. In 1730, ninety-seven Freemasons in the lodges of the Grand Lodge of London were members or future members of the Royal Society. Almost none are found in the Grand Lodge of Ancients, founded in 1751.[13]

As we have seen earlier, Moray, along with Hamilton, Ashmole, and Mainwaring, as well as Henri Pritchard and Edouard Hall, were received into Masonry before the time of Freemasonry.*

Taking his proof further, Boutin points out that the structure of the Constitutions of 1723 follows the same pattern as that used by Newton in *Principia*:

- Definition
- Axiom
- Experimentation
- Proposition

The article "Of God and Religion" was analyzed at length along these lines by Rousse-Lacordaire:

*A. R. Hewitt, "The Grand Lodge of England: A History of the First Hundred Years," in a booklet celebrating the 250th anniversary of the founding of the Grand Lodge of England, London, 1967.

Definition:	*A Mason is oblig'd by his Tenure, to obey the moral Law;*
Axiom:	*and if he rightly understands the Art, he will never be a stupid Atheist, nor an irreligious Libertine.*
Experimentation:	*But though in ancient Times Masons were charg'd in every Country to be of the Religion of that Country or Nation, whatever it was,*
Proposition:	*yet 'tis now thought more expedient only to oblige them to that Religion in which all Men agree, leaving their particular Opinions to themselves; that is, to be good Men and true, or Men of Honour and Honesty, by whatever Denominations or Persuasions they may be distinguish'd; whereby Masonry becomes the Center of Union, and the Means of conciliating true Friendship among Persons that must else have remain'd at a perpetual Distance.*

How could we forget that this text was written by James Anderson—a Presbyterian puritan and defender of trinitarian orthodoxy—yet under the vigilant attention of the liberal Reverend Desaguliers, whose theological ideas were very close to those of Newton?

In their works published in 1993[14] in memory of René Buvet, the Brothers of the Grand Orient of France quoted this famous line from Alexander Pope: "Nature and Nature's laws lay hid in night: God said, 'Let Newton be!' and all was light." They also emphasized the connection between Newton and Locke, who in his "Treatise of Civil Government" in 1690 allowed the theological justification for a contractual monarchy.

Amid the proliferation of Rosicrucians and scientists at the end of the seventeenth century, Newton performed a prodigious interpretation of the Book of Revelation, at the extreme of the limits of what the Church would tolerate. He weaves a thread allowing theology to be enriched by the study of natural laws, without opposing the official God, yet also allowing for freedom and progress.

Using this compromise as support, Desaguliers organized a social and political force that avoided confrontation and, always staying along the edges, managed to gain new territory. Wary of extremist preachers, nascent Freemasonry took in "dissenters" and Huguenot refugees.[15] In 1764, Reverend Davenport, in a famous sermon, was heard explaining that new Brothers should be accepted with prudence, and that, at the same time . . . the Lodges should be opened to women!

There is still much controversy over the existence of Hanoverian and Jacobite Freemasonry, and over the prevarications that led the Vatican to forbid membership in the Order in 1738.[16] Many hypotheses remain to be elucidated, confirmed, or refuted. In any case, we shall stick to the course of the current demonstration.

Starting in the Masonic Lodges of Scotland, the accepted Masons, partisans of Charles I, traveled, studied, and spread their influence enough to create places for research and debate in a war-torn nation. Their creations, with the aid of Rosicrucians, Hermeticists, alchemists, scientists, and politicians, allowed them to build the foundations of what would become Freemasonry just after the beginning of the eighteenth century. This cocktail was favorable, and produced the text of 1723, based on a successful political reconciliation of Cromwellians and Royalists. English Freemasonry, born of Scots and dissidents, sealed the compromise of the Restoration and Parliamentarianism.

History is made from small events and great accomplishments. That of Freemasonry remains to be constructed, clarified, and interpreted. We do not wish to demonstrate anything for eternity, or to create a new catechism. Nobody, not even the most fundamentalist Freemasons, should forget that in the true lodges, there are neither sacraments nor clergy. There one does not conduct worship; one seeks the truth.

Philippe Muray, in his remarkable book *Le XIXe siècle à travers les âges*, writes of the point at which we would like to believe in a denatured, instrumentalist history, free from contradictions and paradoxes.[17] The nineteenth century appears as an inexorable pursuit of the curious relations between science and alchemy, magic and reason, occultism and progress. Victor Hugo turned some tables, Auguste Comte created a religion, Blanqui wrote about the eternity of the stars. . . . The complexity of research struggled against the ambient simplism.

We have long believed the age of information to be liberating. Our society has become one of entertainment and spectacles: the emptiness of prime-time television, the frantic search for a show as the aseptic product of almighty consumption. Freemasonry was created in order to understand complexity, to accept differences, to gather and pose questions, while at the same time trying to provide, here and there, solutions or tools useful for those who are willing to use them.

The Freemasonry of Newton and the Newtonians is as alive as it was on the first day. Our goal has been, almost three centuries after the self-willed birth of the Order—a birth attended by multiple parents—to affirm the freedom of research and the necessity for questioning, both for our history and for our contemporary actions.

Newton was not the image of the statue that the scientific world has erected for him. In all his contradictions, his opposition to Cartesianism, and his theological "delusions," the freedom of thought can always be seen showing through.

The Royal Society preceded him, incorporated him, and changed him as much as it influenced him. The role of Desaguliers was essential.

We find nothing that indicates to us that we have reason to believe in our hypothesis. But at least it is proposed to the reader as a tool of his own conviction. Secularism has never been an excuse for ignorance. The research continues.

Some final morsels of history: Saint-Germain-en-Laye appears to have been the emblematic meeting place of the Jacobites after 1649. Robert Moray was there; hundreds of Stuartists took refuge there in 1688; and in 1737, Bertin du Recheret wrote that "[T]his old English society was introduced into France following James II in 1689." Considering that Newton's scientific discoveries are symbolized by an apple, it is appropriate that one of the lodges that formed the Grand Lodge of London in 1717 was located in the tavern known as the Apple Tree.

AFTERWORD

By Roger Dachez, President of the Masonic Institute of France

After coming to the end of these pages, I imagine the attentive reader being gripped by mixed and contradictory sentiments. On the one hand, the reader will have the confusing feeling of no longer being able to discern the real nature of Freemasonry, seen in the light of such a heavily revised and corrected history; one will also have seen, in the course of reading, the extreme complexity of the subject, belying the simplified images with which we have so long been inundated. But on the other hand, it will probably appear to him that in blazing the trail, following the strenuous paths of research, their detours, and their unexpected pitfalls, we have come to a new stage in the journey, without any definite doubts. Henceforth we have at our disposal almost all the elements necessary for finally penetrating the most important mystery of Freemasonry: that of its origins.

Afterword

A few years ago, the subject to which Alain Bauer has dedicated his work might have appeared relatively simple, using little more than a few medieval manuscripts and a few of Anderson's printed pages. But recently, everything has changed. Numerous works, initially in Great Britain, then in France, have emerged to topple fragile certainties, comfortable hypotheses, and reassuring constructions. When an institution, whatever it might be, experiences such an overhaul in terms of its historical foundations and its traditional sources, the critical work often meets with lively resistance. People willingly cry spiritual treason or proclaim intellectual confusion, if not indeed conspiracy! The very vigor of such reactions—I was a witness to, and to a certain extent the object of, such things a few years ago—shows how high the stakes are.

A group's memory can never be questioned with impunity, especially when it is a matter of the transmission of this memory—in a word its *tradition*, the very essence of its life and the justification for its existence. We must acknowledge, somewhat bitterly, the resistance exhibited by certain Masonic circles in the face of new theories on the origins of Masonry. It is curiously reminiscent of the dominant attitude in Catholic thought when, at the turn of the nineteenth and twentieth centuries, the critical approach to the Scriptures and to the origins of Christianity, in the wake of Renan and Loisy, led to the violent crisis of "modernism." Thus, Masonry, in almost three centuries of existence, has not entirely escaped the pitfall of a certain intellectual conformism.

But this is unimportant. The work of establishing a new corpus of our founding memories has now advanced enough that prudent syntheses can finally be proposed. Heuristic tools and provisional theories allow us to make salutary use of the knowledge now obtained and the problems remaining unsolved. It is on this terrain, where few risks are taken, that Alain Bauer has made advances. Using abundant literature—of which the many references in the book give testimony—this work possesses, in my view, great value as a summary, and can be used as a guide for clearing the convoluted paths leading to the birth of Freemasonry. Let us review the essential stages.

It has been firmly established that the myths relating to the directly operative origins of Freemasonry, seeing the cathedral builders as the true forerunners of speculative Masons and viewing these latter as legitimate heirs of the former, can no longer be considered as anything more than what they are: myths—that is to say, stories that are significant but are in no way historical facts. One might, incidentally, question the use of the word *myth* to designate the literary tableaux that set the stage for the "*œuvriers*" and the "*imagiers*" and instead use the word *legend*. However, I will stick with *myth* and will not hesitate to quote Mircea Eliade:

> This sacred history—mythology—is exemplary: it tells how things came into being, but it also defines all human behaviors and all social and cultural institutions.[1]

Thus, the "History of the Craft," which forms the main part of the "Old Charges"—the sacred history, which some might call the "holy history"—is factually erroneous but profound and rich in meaning. From the fifteenth century on, the Craft, and later its new branch, speculative Masonry, whose annals Anderson laboriously compiled and connected in his Constitutions, did nothing but pass on its myths. Because it was entirely free from all historical equivocation, the Masons were able to readapt it as an object of meditation, as a symbol to explore, as a traditional metaphor.

The event may seem minor, but it is decisive. Ceasing to search for the key to understanding itself in mysterious and abstruse geometry and in the fabulous architectonic legacy of the pyramids, speculative Masonry can now redirect its attention to what, after almost three centuries, defines it and gives it structure: an intellectual and moral adventure.

For only now does the real work of rebuilding begin, as I mentioned earlier: now that the founding myth has been in no way dispelled but rather set in its proper place, it must be substituted with an account of the origins. The present work, without making any conclusions on the origins since so many paths yet remain to explore, does well in defining the places from which one can assume the first sparks of speculative Masonry to have burst forth: they can be found in the intellectual, political, and religious history of Europe in the late Renaissance and the seventeenth century. This new perspective, it seems, need not be called into question any more.

If we summarize broadly, many currents of thought surface immediately:

- The architectural theory of the Renaissance—which, above all, took its "lessons from the ruins"—whose foundations were laid by the great Italian treaties of the fifteenth century

- The Rosicrucian movement, whose significance we cannot ignore, from the work of Frances Yates to that of Roland Edighoffer, inseparable from the political and religious conflicts of Europe at the end of the sixteenth century, and also accounting for the Masonic history of Elias Ashmole and Robert Moray
- The radical change of the physical paradigm with the Newtonian revolution—continuing, at the end of the seventeenth century
- The work of Copernicus from over a hundred years earlier, as the studies of Alexandre Koyré have established—and of which the Royal Society was the crowning achievement in England
- The final unavoidable emergence, at the turn of the eighteenth century, of the concept of tolerance, and, correspondingly, that of sociability, of which Locke and Desaguliers were two prophets in England, the country celebrated by Voltaire in 1734, in his *Lettres Philosophiques*, as the Promised Land of the political and religious freedom that would finally spread throughout Europe and establish our modern society

All these intellectual movements and their key players were involved, as Alain Bauer pertinently points out, in the first manifestations of the speculative Masonry of which they were the very creators. It is here that one must draw on the fundamental references of Masonry and research the significance that it places on its symbols, as well as the meaning it gives to its progress.

Now, the adoption of these new historical references is of considerable importance in my opinion, because they testify that the climate in which speculative Masonry was born was that of an authentic revolution of the spirit. Has it been sufficiently remarked that all the documentary data relating to speculative Masonry increasingly point toward the last quarter of the seventeenth century, reaching their climax in the symbolic act constituted by the founding, in 1717, of the Grand Lodge of London? Has it been observed that the aforesaid period was precisely the period that Paul Hazard, in research completely independent from Masonic history, identified—specifically, according to him, between 1680 and 1715—as the historic era of the European crisis of conscience? Does not this extraordinary coincidence deserve our attention?

In concluding his in-depth study, summarizing the "thirty-five years of the intellectual life of Europe," Hazard writes:

> Everything that is, is a microcosm of the whole. We know that. We know, too, that there is nothing new under the sun, for have we not been trying all along to trace relationships and construct genealogies? But if we are to give the name "novelty," "new" (and that seems the nearest the intellectual department is able to supply)—if we are to apply the word "new" to something which, after a long period of germination, comes finally to birth, or to a fresh manifestation of eternal forces which, long dormant, burst forth anew and with a blaze so sudden and so dazzling as to seem new to ignorant or forgetful men; or if, again, we apply the term "new" to a particular tone, a particular way of saying things; or to a

> resolve to look forward rather than back, to discard the past after winning from it all we can; if, finally, we call "new" an intellectual movement so dynamic as notably to influence our everyday lives, then something new indeed, a change whose effects have lasted right down to our times, was wrought during those years when certain men of genius—Spinoza, Bayle, Locke, Newton, Bossuet, Fénelon, to name only the most illustrious—addressed themselves to the task of exploring the whole field of knowledge in order to bring out the verities which govern and condition the life of man. Applying to the moral sphere what one of them, Leibniz, said of the political, we, too, may say: *Finis saeculi novam rerum faciem aperuit*: in the closing years of the XVIIth century a new order of things began its course.[2]

Speculative Masonry was obviously a sign and a relay of this "new order of things," if not one of the causes—and a clear understanding of this origin is surely necessary for the correct comprehension of the Masonic universe, today even more than in the past.

Appendix 1

SUMMARY OF THE HISTORY OF FREEMASONRY

THE MYTHOLOGICAL-ROMANTIC VERSION (ACCORDING TO ANDERSON)

2247 BC Noah saves the traditions and transmits them to the world

2188 BC Mizraim, son of Ham, transmits the Royal Art into Egypt

1490 BC Transmission of the Royal Art to Moses

1111 BC Building of the Temple of Solomon

586 BC Destruction of the Temple by Nebuchadnezzar

536 BC Decree of Cyrus authorizes the reconstruction of the Temple

515 BC	Transmission of the Royal Art into Greece
352 BC	Building of the Mausoleum at Helicarnassus
304 BC	Euclid redefines geometry
256 BC	Building of the Tower of Pharos by Pharaoh Ptolemeus Philadelphus
1st c. BC	Augustus Caesar is Grand Master of the Lodge of Rome
1st c. BC	Vitruvius
57 BC	Destruction of the second Temple of Jerusalem
448 AD	The Saxons and Scots discover the Royal Art
741	Charles Martel sends architects to England
930	King Athelstan of England creates lodges modeled on those of the French Masons present in England; his son Edwin, a Master Mason, founds the General Lodge of York
1066	Normans are victorious in England
1362	Henry Yevele is the King's Freemason under Edward III
1425	Henry VI forbids general assemblies of Masons
1603	Union of the Kingdoms; Masonry revived by James VI
1717	Founding of the Grand Lodge of London
1723	Anderson's Constitutions
1725	Founding of the Grand Lodge of York
1753	Founding of the Grand Lodge of Ancients
1813	Founding of the United Grand Lodge of England

THE SCIENTIFIC VERSION

1356	Founding of the Company of Masons of London
1390	Regius poem is written
1410	Cooke manuscript is written
1583	Grand Lodge manuscript is written
1598	Schaw Statutes are issued
1641	Robert Moray is accepted
1647	Elias Ashmole is accepted
1688	First lodge founded in France
1717	Founding of the Grand Lodge of London
1723	Anderson's Constitutions
1725	Founding of the Grand Lodge of York
1728	Founding of the first Grand Lodge in France
1730	Adoptive Masonry emerges in France
1738	Publication of Ramsay's "Discourse" and a revised edition of Anderson's Constitutions
1750	Founding, in England, of the Royal Order of Scotland Heredom of Kilwinning
1753	Founding of the Grand Lodge of Ancients
1754	Publication of *Ahiman Rezon* by Laurence Dermott
1765	Étienne Morin distributes a rite of perfection in 256 degrees at Saint-Domingue
1773	Organization of the Grand Orient of France
1813	Union of the Grand Lodges of Ancients and Moderns
1929	Invention of the landmarks

Appendix 2

THE GRAND MASTERS OF ENGLAND

THE GRAND MASTERS OF THE GRAND LODGE OF ENGLAND

The Mythical Version

287	St. Alban, King
557	St. Augustine, Archbishop of Canterbury
597	Austin, monk
680	Bennet, Abbot of Wirral
856	St. Swithin
872	King Alfred the Great
900	Ethred, King of Mercia
	Prince Ethelward

924	King Athelstan
925	Prince Edwin
957	St. Dunstan, Archbishop of Canterbury
1041	King Edward the Confessor
	Leofric, Earl of Coventry
1066	Roger of Montgomery, Earl of Arundel
	Gundulph, Archbishop of Rochester
1100	King Henry I
1135	Gilbert de Clare, Earl of Pembroke
1154	Bernard de Tremblay, Grand Master of the Templars
1176	Peter de Colechurch
1212	William Almaine
1216	Peter de Rupibus, Archbishop of Winchester
1234	Geoffrey Fitz Peter
1272	Walter Giffard, Archbishop of York
	Gilbert de Clare, Earl of Gloucester
	Ralph, Lord of Mount Hermer
1307	Walter Stapleton, Archbishop of Exeter
1327	King Edward III
1350	John de Spoulee, Master of the Ghiblim
1357	William of Wickham, Archbishop of Winchester
1375	Robert Barnham
	Henry Yevele, the King's Freemason
	Simon Langham, Abbot of Westminster
1377	William of Wickham (second term)
1399	Thomas Fitz Allen, Earl of Surrey
1413	Henry Chicheley, Archbishop of Canterbury
1443	William Waynflete, Archbishop of Winchester

1471	Richard Beauchamp, Archbishop of Salisbury
1485	King Henry VII
1493	John Islip, Abbot of Westminster
1502	Sir Reginald Bray
1515	Cardinal Thomas Wolsey
1539	Thomas Cromwell, Earl of Essex
1540	Lord John Touchett
1549	Edward Seymour, Duke of Somerset
1550	John Poynet, Archbishop of Winchester
1561	Sir Thomas Sackville
1567	Francis Russell, Earl of Bedford
	Sir Thomas Gresham
1579	Charles Howard, Earl of Effingham
1588	George Hastings, Earl of Huntingdon
1603	King James I
1607	Inigo Jones, architect
1618	William Herbert, Earl of Pembroke
1625	King Charles I
1630	Henry Danvers, Earl of Danby
1633	Thomas Howard, Earl of Arundel
1634	Francis Russell, Earl of Bedford
1635	Inigo Jones (second term)
1660	King Charles II
	Henry Jermyn, Earl of St. Albans
1666	Thomas Savage, Earl of Rivers
1674	George Villars, Duke of Buckingham
1679	Henry Bennett, Earl of Arlington
1685	Sir Christopher Wren

1695 Charles Lenox, Duke of Richmond
1698 Sir Christopher Wren (second term)

The Historical Version

1717 Anthony Sayer, lawyer
1718 George Payne, historian
1719 John Theophilus Desaguliers, doctor of theology, Newton's secretary
1720 George Payne (second term)
1721 John, Duke of Montague
1722 Philip, Duke of Wharton
1723 Francis Scott, Earl of Dalkeith
1724 Charles Lenox, Duke of Richmond
1725 Lord James Hamilton
1726 William O'Brien, Earl of Inchiquin
1727 Lord Henry Hare
1728 Lord James King
1729 Thomas Howard, Duke of Norfolk
1731 Lord Novel
1732 Anthony Brown, Viscount Montagu
1733 James Lyon, Earl of Strathmore
1734 John Lindsay, Earl of Crawford

THE GRAND MASTERS OF THE GRAND LODGE OF YORK

1725 Charles Bathurst
1729 Edward Thompson

1733	John Johnson
1734	John Marsden
1792	The Grand Lodge of York is dissolved

THE GRAND MASTERS OF THE GRAND LODGE OF ANCIENTS

1753	Robert Turner
1754	Edward Vaughan
1756	The Earl of Blessington
1813	The Grand Lodge of Ancients merges with the Grand Lodge

THE GRAND MASTERS OF THE GRAND LODGE OF SCOTLAND

1736	William Sinclair of Roslyn
1737	George, Earl of Cromarty
1738	John, Earl of Kintore
1739	James, Earl of Morton
1740	Thomas, Earl of Strathmore and Kinghorn
1741	Alexander, Earl of Leven and Melville
1742	William, Earl of Kilmarnock
1743	James, Earl of Wemyss

Appendix 3

TIMELINE OF EVENTS LEADING TO THE GRAND LODGE OF ENGLAND

1066	William the Conqueror victorious over Harold II at the Battle of Hastings; England becomes a centralized Anglo-Norman kingdom
1072	William forces Malcolm III, king of Scotland, to pay him homage
1080	William declares to the bishop of Rome that the king of England owes him no homage
1086	Establishment of the land register in England
1087	William dies during the Norman revolt
1087	William II becomes king; war of succession between the sons of William I

1100	Henry I becomes king of England
1117	Norman rebellion
1118	Founding of the Order of the Temple
1122	Normal rebellion
1135	Matilda becomes queen of England
1154	Henry II becomes king of England
1164	Constitutions of Clarendon restrict the jurisdiction of church tribunals; opposition of royal councilor Thomas à Becket
1170	Thomas à Becket, Archbishop of Canterbury, is assassinated
1171	Conquest of Ireland
1189	Richard I the Lionheart becomes king of England
1199	John becomes king of England
1207	The king refuses to accept the new archbishop of Canterbury; England is served in interdict by the pope
1209	King John is excommunicated by the pope
1213	The interdict is lifted and ties with Rome are reestablished
1215	Revolt against John Lackland; Magna Carta
1216	Henry III becomes king of England
1264	Simon de Montfort overthrows Henry III
1265	Founding of the House of Commons; Simon de Montfort is defeated
1272	Edward I becomes king of England
1283	Conquest of Wales
1290	The Jews are expelled

1291	Edward I is sovereign of Scotland
1295	Reestablishment of Parliament
1297	Scotland secedes
1298	Scotland is reconquered
1306	Scotland secedes
1307	Edward II becomes king of England
1312	The Order of the Temple is abolished
1313	Scotland is independent
1326	Edward II is deposed by Parliament and then assassinated
1327	Edward III becomes king of England
1333	Scotland is reconquered
1337	Beginning of the Hundred Years' War with France (ends in 1453)
1348	Great Plague; a third of the population dies
1377	Richard II becomes king of England
1381	Peasants' Revolt
1399	Richard II is deposed, Henry IV becomes king of England
1413	Henry V becomes king of England
1422	Henry VI becomes king of England, Regency until 1437
1454	Regency due to the king's mental illness
1455	Henry VI restored
1460	Defeat at Wakefield, Henry VI captured
1461	Edward IV becomes king of England
1470	Restoration of Henry VI
1471	Restoration of Edward IV

1483	Richard III becomes king of England
1485	Defeat and death of Richard III
1486	Henry VII becomes king of England
1509	Henry VIII becomes king of England
1513	Scots defeated; King James IV of Scotland dies
1521	Henry VIII is proclaimed "Defender of the Faith" by the pope
1529	Breakaway from Rome begins; Thomas More is lord chancellor
1533	Excommunication
1534	Act of Supremacy; schism with the Catholic Church; the Church of England is established
1535	Thomas More is executed
1536	Dissolution of the monasteries in England
1539	Bill of Six Articles states the principles of Catholic dogma
1547	Edward VI becomes king of England
1549	Introduction of Protestantism into England
1553	Jane Grey is queen for nine days; deposed by Queen Mary I Tudor
1554	Catholicism reestablished; Protestants are persecuted
1558	Elizabeth I becomes queen
1559	Act of Uniformity reestablishes the Church of England
1567	Mary Queen of Scots is forced to abdicate in favor of James VI
1587	Mary Queen of Scots is executed
1588	The English defeat the Spanish Armada

1597	Irish rebellion
1603	James VI of Scotland (Protestant) becomes King James I of England
1605	Gunpowder Plot
1618	The Thirty Years' War begins
1622	Parliament is dissolved
1625	Charles I, son of James I, becomes king of England
1628	Petition of Right
1638	Union of the opposition under the name of the Covenant; civil and religious war
1640	War with Parliament; rebellion in Ireland
1642	The king orders the arrest of the leaders of the opposition, who take refuge in the City of London, which refuses to hand them over; beginning of the Civil War with the "Roundheads," led by Cromwell
1645	Cromwell victorious over royal troops; Charles I hands himself over to the Scots
1648	The Scots are defeated; Treaty of Westphalia ends war
1649	Charles I is executed
1650	Charles II becomes king of Scotland; invades England; is defeated
1653	Cromwell becomes Lord Protector; dictatorship
1658	Cromwell dies
1659	Stuarts restored; Charles II becomes king
1662	Act of Uniformity
1665	Great Plague; of the 500,000 inhabitants of London, 75,000 die

1666	Great Fire of London
1679	*Habeas corpus* voted in by Parliament
1681	Parliament dissolved
1685	James II becomes king of England and Scotland
1687	Act of Tolerance; freedom of conscience and religion
1688	"Glorious Revolution" against the Roman Catholics; William III and Mary II become king and queen of England and Scotland
1689	James II accepts Bill of Rights under pressure from Parliament; he takes refuge in Saint-Germain-en-Laye after his military defeat
1694	Queen Mary dies
1701	The War of the Spanish Succession begins
1702	Anne becomes queen of England
1707	Act of Union between England and Scotland
1713	Treaty of Utrecht; War of the Spanish Succession ends
1714	George I becomes king of England
1715	Jacobite rebellion in Scotland
1717	Founding of the Grand Lodge of London
1725	Founding of the Grand Lodge of York
1727	George II becomes king
1740	War of Austrian Succession
1745	Jacobite rebellion in Scotland
1753	Founding of the Grand Lodge of York
1756	Seven Years' War begins
1760	George III becomes king of England
1763	Treaty of Paris ends the Seven Years' War

1773 Boston Tea Party
1775 War of Independence begins in America
1813 Founding of the United Grand Lodge of England

Appendix 4

TIMELINE OF EVENTS LEADING TO THE GRAND LODGE OF FRANCE

987	Hugh Capet becomes king of France
996	Robert II becomes king of France
997	Robert is excommunicated for bigamy
1031	Henry I becomes king of France
1031	Civil wars against the great feudal lords (until 1039)
1060	Philip I becomes king of France
1096	First Crusade
1100	Philip is excommunicated for bigamy
1108	Louis VI becomes king of France
1137	Louis VII becomes king of France
1147	Second Crusade

1159 Beginning of the first Hundred Years' War with the Plantagenets of Anjou, the kings of England, and the Capetiens; Louis VII becomes king of France
1180 Philip August becomes king of France
1189 Third Crusade
1199 Philip is served an interdict for irregular marriage
1202 Fourth Crusade
1208 War with the Albigensians begins
1212 Children's Crusade
1214 Battle of Bouvines
1217 Fifth Crusade
1223 Louis VIII becomes king of France
1226 Louis IX (St. Louis) becomes king of France; Regency until 1239
1228 Sixth Crusade
1230 Crusade of the Barons
1248 Seventh Crusade
1251 Shepherds' Crusade; Jews are persecuted in France
1270 Eighth Crusade; Philip III becomes king of France
1285 Philip IV the Fair becomes king of France
1298 First Hundred Years' War ends
1300 Albigensian uprising
1302 First States-General; affirmation of royal power against the pope
1306 Confiscation of the holdings of the Jews in Lombardy
1314 Louis X becomes king of France

1315	Emancipation of the serfs in the royal domain
1316	John I becomes king of France
1316	Philip V becomes king of France
1322	Charles IV becomes king of France
1328	Philip VI of Valois becomes king of France
1347	The Plague; 50 percent of the French population dies
1350	John II becomes king of France
1355	States-General at Paris; grand ordinance limits royal power
1356	John II taken prisoner by the English (for four years)
1358	States-General revoked; Jacques Bonhomme's revolt
1360	Decree of Compiègne creates the franc
1364	Charles V becomes king of France
1378	Great Schism; two popes are elected
1380	Charles VI becomes king of France; Regency of Louis I of Anjou
1382	Revolts against the tax
1393	The king has fits of madness; Regency
1394	The Jews are expelled
1399	Plague epidemic
1422	Charles VII becomes king of France; France is occupied by the English; Treaty of Troyes
1431	Henry VI of England is crowned king of France in Paris
1436	Liberation of Paris by Charles VII
1437	"Pragmatic Sanction of Bourges"; establishment of a permanent royal army; Revolt of the Nobles
1461	Louis XI becomes king of France

1465	Revolt of the Nobles
1467	Revolt of the Nobles
1468	States-General
1472	Revolt of the Nobles
1483	Charles VIII becomes king of France
1598	Edict of Nantes
1685	Revocation of the Edict of Nantes
1688	First lodge in France
1728	Founding of the first Grand Lodge in France; Philip Duke of Wharton is named first Grand Master
1773	Unification of the Grand Orient of France; formation of other Obediences, Central Grand Lodge, Supreme Council, and Symbolic Scottish Grand Lodge
1501	Suspension of the fraternities of the masons and carpenters
1538	The personal guard of the king of France is Scottish
1539	Francis I, in the Decree of Villers-Cotterêts, abolishes the companies claiming ancient rights and attempts to demolish all the guilds and companies
1562	Beginning of the religious wars in France
1572	Massacre of Saint Bartholomew
1574	Formation of the Calvinist Union in France
1598	Edict of Nantes gives Protestants the freedom of conscience; this can be considered one of the first historical acts of secularism

1614	Last States-General in France before the Revolution
1616	Richelieu joins the King's Council
1628	Richelieu is victorious in the siege of La Rochelle
1629	The Peace of Alès ends the political power of the Protestants in France
1641	Robert Moray is received at St. Mary's Chapel
1645	The clergy suspects guild (Compagnonnage) meetings and forbids its members to participate in guild assemblies, under penalty of expulsion
1659	Peace of the Pyrenees
1685	Louis XIV revokes the Edict of Nantes; 300,000 people are exiled from France, among them the Desaguliers family
1687	Newton releases his work on the principles of universal gravitation
1721	The contested founding of the first English lodge in France, at Dunkirk: the Amitié et Fraternité (Friendship and Brotherhood) of the Grand Lodge of England
1725	Four lodges are recorded in France (in a Grand Orient of France circular of September 4, 1788): Louis d'Argent, de Bussy et d'Aumont, de la Parfaite Union, and de Benouville
1726	Coustos Villeroy Lodge founded in Paris by John Meyer Coustos, an English lapidary
1728	Founding of the first Grand Lodge in France; Philip, Duke of Wharton, is its first Grand Master; founding of the Ramsay system, with seven degrees

1730 Emergence of women's Masonry in France, which is in fact Adoptive Masonry, sponsored by the male lodges

1735 French translation of Anderson's Constitutions by the Irish abbot Moore; six masonic lodges exist in Paris

1736 Foundation of the Loge Saint-Jean-d'Écosse de la Vertu Persécutée, Scottish Mother Lodge of Avignon

1737 Presumed first appearance of the word *freemason*

1738 The Duke d'Antin is the second French Grand Master; emergence of the Ordre mixte paramaçonnique des Mopses (Mixed Paramasonic Order of the Mopses)

1742 There are twenty-two lodges in Paris, and more than two hundred outside the capital (according to Thory)

1760 Willermoz gains the approval of the Grand Lodge of France to found the Grand Lodge of Regular Masters of Lyons; development of the Rite of Adoption

1762 Jesuits banished from France

1764 Louis XV outlaws the Company of Jesus

1765 Birth of Grasse-Tilly

1766 Louis XV dissolves all Masonic lodges; Ordre de l'Étoile Flamboyante (Order of the Flaming Star) is created by Baron de Tschoudy; Lorraine is returned to France; Anglaise Lodge opens in Bordeaux, receiving a patent from the First Grand Lodge

1769 First chapter of Rose Croix is founded in Paris

1771 Louis-Philippe d'Orléans, the Duke of Chartres (the future Philippe Égalité), is elected Grand Master and Protector of all lodges in France

1773 May 24: Founding of the Grand Orient of France by the Grand Lodge of France and all the Venerable Masters of the independent lodges, including the adoptive lodges

1782 Official creation of the Chamber of Degrees by the Grand Orient of France; codification of the French Rite by Roettiers de Montaleau, with the Régulateur du Maçon

1804 Napoleon Bonaparte is crowned emperor of France as Napoleon I; Grasse-Tilly assembles a provisional Supreme Council for France from the Ancient and Accepted Scottish Rite; codification of the Ancient and Accepted Scottish Rite by the publication of the Guide for Scottish Masons; inspiration of the "Three Distinct Knocks"

1809 The Grand Orient of France authorizes the lodges to practice several rites

1840 Freemasonry adopts the motto "Liberté, Égalité, Fraternité" (Liberty, Equality, Fraternity) in the lodges

1849 The First Constitution of the Masonic Order in France is voted in at Convention of the Grand Orient of France (before, there were only statutes)

1853 The Grand Orient of France moves to its present location at 16 rue Cadet

1864 Last meeting of the adoptive lodge of Jérusalem des Vallées Égyptiennes (from this date onward, there is no women's adoptive Freemasonry until 1901)

1877 At the impulse of Pastor Frédéric Desmons, the Convention of the Grand Orient of France votes to abolish the requirement of belief in God and the immortality of the soul

1880 Founding of the Symbolic Grand Lodge of Scotland, created from twelve lodges of the Supreme Council of France

1882 Initiation of the woman of letters Maria Deraisme into the Lodge Les Libres Penseurs (The Free Thinkers) at Pecq, from the Symbolic Grand Lodge of Scotland

1887 Official secularization of the rituals of the French Rite

1893 Maria Deraisme initiates six women and creates, along with Georges Martin, a mixed Obedience, the Droit Humain (Human Right), which practices the Ancient and Accepted Scottish Rite

1894 The Supreme Council creates the Grand Lodge of France

1896 The Symbolic Grand Lodge of Scotland is assimilated into the Grand Lodge of France

1901 Resurgence of women's adoptive lodges under the tutelage of the Grand Lodge of France, with the lodge Le Libre Examen, sponsored by the male lodge of the same name

1905	Separation of Church and State
1913	Founding of the Grand Loge Indépendante et Régulière pour la France et les Colonies françaises (Regular and Independent Grand Lodge for France and the French Colonies) by Édouard de Ribaucourt; It takes the name National Grand Lodge of France in 1948
1945	Women's adoptive Masonry is discarded by the Grand Lodge of France (still with the hope of a Masonic recognition by the United Grand Lodge of England); thanks to the energy of a small group of sisters, a specific women's Masonry is established for the first time under the name Union Maçonnique Féminine de France (Women's Masonic Union of France)
1946	Beginning of the Fourth Republic
1952	The Women's Masonic Union of France changes its name to the Grande Loge Féminine de France (Women's Grand Lodge of France)
1958	Beginning of the Fifth Republic; founding of the Grand Loge Nationale Française-Opéra, which then changes its name to the Grand Loge Traditionnelle et Symbolique-Opéra
1959	The Women's Grand Lodge of France abandons the Rite of Adoption to practice the Ancient and Accepted Scottish Rite
1968	Founding of the Loge Nationale Française by René Guilly

1973 Founding of the Grand Loge Mixte Universelle, whose members came from the Droit Humain

1981 Founding of the Grand Loge Mixte de France (Mixed Grand Lodge of France)

Appendix 5

DIALOGUE BETWEEN SIMON, A TOWN MASON, AND PHILIP, A TRAVELING MASON

This manuscript is a kind of catechism summarizing the essential customs and modes of recognition of Masons in London around 1730. It is interesting in particular because of its evocation, especially in the enigmatic drawings that accompany it, of the "Desaguliers regulation," perhaps referring to certain decisions made by the Grand Lodge in August 1730 in order to protect against false Masons.

In any case, it shows that some Masons had established a distinction between Masonry before Desaguliers and Masonry after him.

This source, which merits a longer study, allows us to determine the point at which Desaguliers' entry into Masonry may have constituted a radical turning point, probably changing the original nature of Masonry quite significantly.

SIMON: Sir, I have just now received enclosed in a letter a piece of paper in this form pray what do you mean by it?

PHILIP: I am a stranger, I want company, and hearing you was a Brother Mason made bold to summons you.

SIMON: And you are a Mason.

PHILIP: I am (so taken to be by all Fellows and Brothers).

SIMON: And how shall I know you to be a Mason.

PHILIP: By Words, Signs, Tokens and Points of my Entrance.

SIMON: And what's the Word of a Mason?

PHILIP: The word is Right.

SIMON: If it be Right give it me Right.

PHILIP: I'll spell it out with you, if you please.

SIMON: Give me the first Letter and I'll give you the second.

PHILIP: B.

SIMON: O.

PHILIP: A.

SIMON: Z.

PHILIP: The Word then is BOAZ, but as you are a stranger to me, as I am to you, and we in good policy are not to answer above Three questions proposed least we should be imposed on by a pretender, I ask you, What are Signs?

Simon: Signs are all Squares, Angles and Perpendiculars.

Philip: And what are the Tokens?

Simon: All Brotherly gripes [grips] on the hand by which Brothers distinguish one another.

Philip: And what are points of your Entrance?

Simon: To Heal and Conceal the Secrets of a Mason.

Philip: How was you admitted a Mason?

Simon: By Three knocks on the Door the last at a double distance of time from the former and much larger.

Philip: What was the first question that the Master ask'd you when you was admitted?

Simon: Whither it was of my own free will that I came thither to be made a Mason. I answered Yes.

Philip: What did you see before you was made a Mason?

Simon: Nothing that I understood.

Philip: What did you see afterwards?

Simon: Three grand Lights.

Philip: What do you call them?

Simon: The Sun, the Moon, and the Master.

Philip: How do they rule and govern?

Simon: The Sun the Day, the Moon the Night, the Master the Lodge.

Philip: Where stood your Master?

Simon: In the East.

Philip: Why in the East?

Simon: To wait the rising of the Sun to set the Men to their Work.

Philip: Where stood the Wardens?

Simon: In the West.

Philip: Why in the West?

Simon: To wait the Setting of the Sun and to discharge the Men from Their Labour.

Philip: Where stood the Fellow Crafts?

Simon: In the South.

Philip: Why in the South?

Simon: To receive and Instruct all strange Brothers.

Philip: Where stood the entered Prentices?

Simon: In the North to Heal and Conceal and wait of the Master.

Philip: You say you see three great Lights, did you see no other Light?

Simon: Yes one far surpassing Sun or Moon.

Philip: What was that?

Simon: The Light of the Gospel.

Philip: Why was you made a Mason?

Simon: For the sake of the letter G.

Philip: What does it signifye?

Simon: Geomitry.

Philip: Why Geomitry?

Simon: Because it is the Root and foundation of all Arts and Sciences.

Philip: And pray how much mony had you in your pocket when you was made a Free Mason?

Simon: None at all.

Philip: And how was you made a Mason?

Simon: Neither Naked nor Cloathed, Standing nor Lying, Kneeling nor Standing, Barfoot nor Shod, but in due form.

Philip: How is that Form?

Simon: Upon my barebended knee with a pair of Compasses extended square in my Breast. And then and there I took the sacred and solemn Oaths of a Mason.

Philip: Repeat your Oaths.

Simon: I do Solemnly Vow and Protest before God and this Worshipful Company that I will Heal or Hear, Conceal and never Reveal the Secrets or Secrecy of a Mason or Masonry that has been heretofore or shall be here or hereafter disclosed unto me, to neither Man, Woman nor Child, neither print them, stamp them or Engrave them or cause them to be written stampt or Engraved upon anything Moveable or Immoveable or any other ways.

Whereby the Secrets or a Mason or Masonry may be discovered. Upon the Penalty of my Heart plucked from my Left breast, my Tongue pluck'd from the roof of my mouth, my Throat cutt, my Body to be torn to pieces by Wild Horses, to by bury'd in the Sands of the Sea where the Tide flowed in 24 Hours, taken up and burn't to Ashes and Sifted where the four winds blow that there may be no more Remembrances of me. SO HELP ME GOD. Then the Senior WARDEN put me on a White apron with these words. I put you on the Badge of a Mason, more Ancient and Honorable than the Knights of the Garter.

PHILIP: I am satisfied you are a Mason by the Repeating of your Oath. If you please you may ask me what Questions you think proper.

SIMON: I ask you where your Lodge was kept.

PHILIP: In the Vale of Jehosophat out of the Cackling of a Hen, the Crowing of a Cock, the barking of a Dog.

SIMON: How high was your Lodge?

PHILIP: As high as the Heavens and as low as the Earth.

SIMON: How many Pillars had your lodge?

PHILIP: Three.

SIMON: What did you call them?

PHILIP: Beauty, Strength, and Wisdom.

SIMON: What do they represent?

PHILIP: Beauty to Adorn, Strength to Support, and Wisdom to Contrive.

SIMON: What Lodge are you of?

Philip: Of the Right Worshipful Lodge of St. John's.

Simon: How many signs has a Free Mason?

Philip: Five.

Simon: What do you call them?

Philip: Pedestal—Manual—Pectoral—Guttural—Oral.

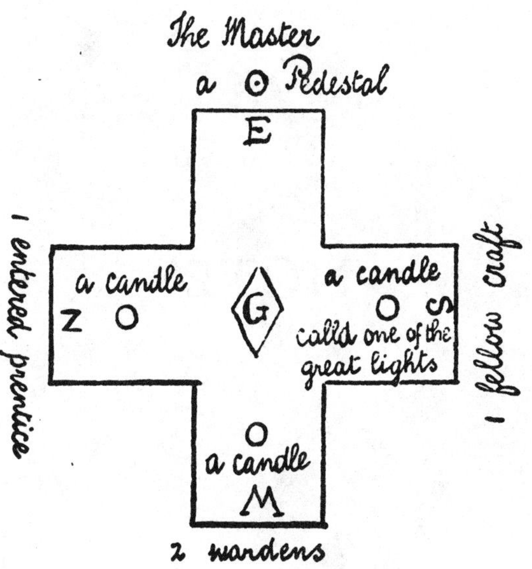

This is the form of the old lodges.

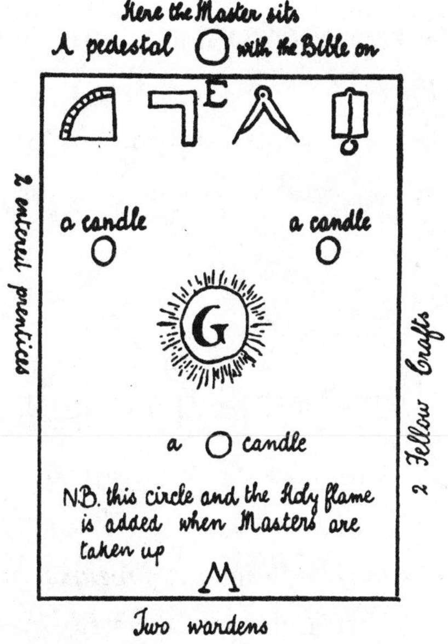

This lodge is the new lodge under the Desaguliers regulations.

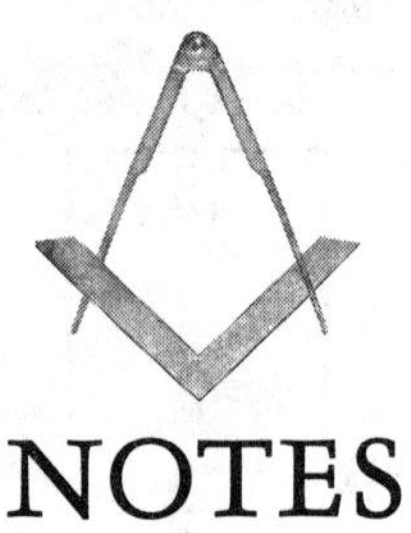

NOTES

INTRODUCTION

1. Alain Bauer, *Grand O,* Denoël, 2001, and Gallimard, coll. "Folio," 2002.
2. Roger Dachez, "Le protestantisme aux origines de la Franc-Maçonnerie," in *Protestantisme et Franc-Maçonnerie* (Edimaf, 2000).

CHAPTER 1
A RETURN TO THE ORIGINS

1. *Actes du IVe Colloque de Renaissance Traditionnelle*, no. 129, January 2002.
2. David Stevenson, *The Origins of Freemasonry: Scotland's Century, 1590–1710* (Cambridge University Press, 1988), xi–xii.

3. René Désaguliers, *Les Pierres de la Franc-Maçonnerie* (Dervy, 1995).
4. Heredom, *The Journal of the Scottish Rite Research Society,* vol. 7, Washington, D.C., 1998.
5. *La Franc-maçonnerie, documents fondateurs,* Cahiers de l'Herne, and *Textes fondateurs de la Tradition maçonnique* (Grasset, 1995).
6. *Kenning's Masonic Encyclopedia and Handbook of Masonic Archeology, History and Biography* (London, 1878).
7. *History of the Grand Lodge of Free and Accepted Masons of Ireland,* vol. 1 (Dublin, 1925).
8. Actes du IVe Colloque de *Renaissance Traditionnelle.*
9. *Illustrations of Masonry,* 1772, with numerous reprints.
10. *Textes fondateurs de la Tradition maçonnique.*
11. W. MacLeod, "The Old Charges and the Hathaway Manuscript," *AQC* 90, 1977, and *AQC* 94, 1981.
12. Cited in C. N. Batham, "La Compagnie des Maçons de Londres," in *Travaux de la Loge Nationale de Recherches Villard de Honnecourt,* series 2, no. 2, 1980.
13. "The Hole Craft and the Fellowship of Masonry," in *AQC,* vol. IX, 1894.
14. Douglas Knoop, G. P. Jones, and Douglas Hamer, *The Medieval Mason* (Manchester, 1967).
15. Harry Carr, "600 Years of Craft Ritual," in *AQC* 81, 1968.
16. Archives of Scotland (SRO), CH.2/198/3, Minutes of the presbytery of Jedburgh, 1644–58, cited by David Stevenson (*The Origins of Freemasonry,* 127–28).

17. Edinburgh University Library, Ms Laing, III, 551 (cited by David Stevenson, 133).
18. *Renaissance Traditionnelle,* no. 47, July 1981.
19. In "The Crisp English Word Freemason," *AQC* 68, 1955.
20. "The Birth of Freemasonry," *AQC* 91, November 1979.
21. Collected in René Désaguliers, *Les Pierres de la Franc-Maçonnerie* (Dervy, 1995).
22. *Renaissance Traditionnelle,* nos. 118–119, April 1999.
23. Cahiers de l'Herne, *La Franc-Maçonnerie, documents fondateurs,* 1992.
24. Patrick Négrier, *Textes fondateurs de la Tradition maçonnique* (Grasser, 1995).
25. Cahiers de l'Herne.
26. *The Origins of Freemasonry,* 26.
27. See *The Origins of Freemasonry,* ch. 3: William Schaw, 26–51.
28. James Anderson, *The Constitutions of the Free-Masons, containing the History, Charges, Regulations, &c. of that most Ancient and Right Worshipful Fraternity* (London, 1723, reprint Philadelphia, 1734).
29. Patrick Négrier, *Textes fondateurs de la Tradition maçonnique.*
30. Ibid.
31. *Ahiman Rezon,* London, 1756, introduction; see also Jean-François Var, "Ahiman Rezon et la Grande Loge des Anciens," in *Travaux de la Loge Nationale de Recherches Villard de Honnecourt,* no. 15.
32. *The Craft* (Crucible, 1986).
33. André Doré, *Vérités et légendes de l'histoire maçonnique* (Edimaf, 1991).

34. José Ferrer Benimellis, "Église et Maçonnerie opérative au Moyen Âge," in *Travaux de la Loge Nationale de Recherches Villard de Honnecourt,* no. 15.
35. See the critique of Paul Naudon's book *Les origines de la Franc-Maçonnerie—Le métier et le Sacré,* in *Renaissance Traditionnelle* 90, April 1992.
36. "Les origines et l'évolution de la Franc-Maçonnerie," in *Travaux de la Loge Nationale de Recherches Villard de Honnecourt,* no. 1, 1980, and "The Origin of Freemasonry: A New Theory," in *AQC* 106, 1993.
37. "Some Thoughts on the Origin of Speculative Masonry," in *AQC* 95, 1982.
38. "The Origin of the Craft," in *AQC* 96, 1983.
39. *Vérités et légendes de l'histoire maçonnique* (Edimaf, 1991).
40. "Les origines de la Maçonnerie spéculative en Grande Bretagne," in *Renaissance Traditionnelle* 77, January 1989, and 83, July 1990.
41. *Renaissance Traditionnelle* 77, January 1989, and 83, July 1990.
42. *Des Maçons opératifs aux Franc-Maçons spéculatifs* (Edimaf, 2001).
43. Our "Algeco."
44. *Renaissance Traditionnelle* 77, 118–119.
45. *How the Scots Invented the Modern World* (New York: Three Rivers Press, 2001).
46. Kervella, *La Passion Écossaise* (Dervy, 2002).
47. Speech at the International Conference of Great Priories, August 2000, and *The Hiram Key* (Arrow, 1997).

48. "Le parfait maçon," publications of the University of Saint-Étienne.
49. Pierre Chevallier, *Le Sceptre, la Crosse et l'Équerre* (Honoré Champion, 1996).
50. Andrew Ramsay, *The Travels of Cyrus,* 4th edition, James Bettenham, London, 1730. See also the French translation, Honoré Champion, 2002, with a preface by Georges Lamoine.
51. Patrick Négrier, *Textes fondateurs de la Tradition maçonnique.*
52. Bernard Quilliet, *La tradition humaniste* (Fayard, 2002).
53. *Des Maçons médiévaux aux compagnons d'aujourd'hui* (Grancher, 2002).

CHAPTER 2
ROBERT MORAY AND THE ROYAL SOCIETY

1. Robert Lomas, *The Invisible College* (London: Headline Books, 2002).
2. David Stevenson, *The Origins of Freemasonry*, and Dudley Wright, "The First Recorded Initiation in England," in *The Builder,* 1921, reprint by Torrione Lodge of Research, no. 34.
3. *The Origins of Freemasonry*, 189.
4. Francis Delon's article "Elias Ashmole, amateur d'antiquités, astrologue, alchimiste et Franc-maçon," in *Travaux de la Loge Nationale de Recherches Villard de Honnecourt*, no. 38, 1998.
5. *The Institutes, Laws and Ceremonies of the Order of the Garter*, 1671.

6. Joan Evans, *An History of the Society of Antiquaries* (Oxford, 1956), and the French synthesis "Les Antiquarians et la Society of Antiquaries," in *Le Jardin des Dragons 12: Les Collèges d'Oxford au XVIIe Siècle*, 97–106.
7. The works of Guy Bernfeld, November 2000.
8. *Le chiffre et le songe, une histoire politique de la découverte* (Odile Jacob, 1993).
9. *Giordano Bruno and the Hermetic Tradition* (London: Routledge, 1961), and *The Rosicrucian Enlightenment* (London: Paladin, 1975).
10. *The Invisible College* (London: Headline Books, 2002), and his speech at the International Conference of Great Priories, August 25, 2000.
11. *The New Jerusalem* (London: Bantam Press, 2002).
12. Jean-Pierre Maury, *Newton et la mécanique céleste* (Découvertes Gallimard, 1990).
13. Jacques Blamont, *Le chiffre et le songe,* 1993.
14. *La Maçonnerie Écossaise dans la France de l'Ancien Régime* and *La Passion Écossaise.*
15. *Des Maçons médiévaux aux compagnons d'aujourd'hui* (Grancher, 2002).
16. Robert Lomas, *The Invisible College* (London: Headline Books, 2002).
17. "La Fondation de la Royal Society," in *Science et Vie*, June 1998.
18. Florence de Lussy, "Un peu de lumière sur les origines anglaises de la Franc-Maçonnerie," in *Revue de la Bibliothèque Nationale* no. 12, Summer 1984.

19. “History of the Royal Society,” in *Record of the Royal Society* (London, 2002).
20. Dwight Atkinson, *Discourse in Sociohistorical Context: The Philosophical Transactions of the Royal Society of London, 1675–1975* (London: Lawrence Erlbaum, 1999).
21. *Directions for Seamen Going into the East and West Indies*, 1666.
22. *Promoting Experimental Learning* (Cambridge University Press, 1991).
23. *Science, Religion, and Belief: The Clerical Virtuosi of the Royal Society of London, 1663–1687* (New York: Peter Lang, 1992).
24. Robert Lomas, *The Invisible College*, 2002.
25. *The City of Revelation* (London: Garnstone Press, 1972).

CHAPTER 3
NEWTON: SCIENTIST, ALCHEMIST, AND SORCERER

1. Tony Allan, *Isaac Newton* (Chicago: Heinemann Library, 2001).
2. Jean-Pierre Maury, *Newton et la mécanique céleste* (Découvertes Gallimard, 1990).
3. *The New Jerusalem*, 2002.
4. *De Magnete* (London, 1600).
5. Jacques Blamont, *Le chiffre et le songe (*Odile Jacob, 1993).
6. *The New Jerusalem*, 2002.

7. The works of Jean-Pierre Chabrol, professor at the IUFM at Marseille.
8. Jean Delumeau, *Mille ans de bonheur: une histoire du paradis* (Fayard, 1995); Clarke Garrett, *Spirit Possession and Popular Religion: From the Camisards to the Shakers* (Baltimore: Johns Hopkins University Press, 1987); and Hillel Schwartz, *The French Prophets* (University of California Press, 1980).
9. *La Malle de Newton* (NRF Gallimard, 1993).
10. *Du monde clos à univers infini* (Gallimard, 1973).
11. *Newton's Prophecies of Daniel* (London, 1733, and reprints, 1991 and 2000).
12. Isaac Newton, *Principia.*
13. *Éléments d'histoire des sciences* (Larousse, 1997).
14. *Zéro: La biographie d'une idée dangereuse* (J.-C. Lattès, 2002).
15. Richard Westfall, *Newton* (Cambridge University Press, 1980 and 1993). See also "The Influence of Alchemy on Newton," in *Science, Pseudo-Science and Society* (Wilfrid Laurier University Press, 1980).
16. *The Foundations of Newton's Alchemy* (Cambridge University Press, 1975), 19.
17. Notably in *An Historical Account of Two Notable Corruptions of Scriptures*, letters to John Locke, 1690.
18. *Memoirs of the Life, Writings and Discoveries of Sir Isaac Newton* (Edinburgh: Thomas Constable, 1855).
19. "Authentic memoirs of Sir Isaac Newton," in *Collections for the History of the Town and Soke of Grantham* (London, 1806).

20. *Memoirs of Sir Isaac Newton's Life*, 1752.
21. *A Portrait of Isaac Newton*, 1968; *The Religion of Isaac Newton*, 1974.
22. *The Foundations of Newton's Alchemy* (Cambridge University Press, 1975).
23. Paolo Rossi, "Hermeticism, Rationality and the Scientific Revolution," in *Reason, Experiment and Mysticism in the Scientific Revolution* (New York: Science History Publications, 1975), 272–73.
24. *Isaac Newton, Adventurer in Thought* (Oxford: Blackwell, 1992), xiv.
25. Especially in *The Newtonian Revolution* (Cambridge University Press, 1980).
26. Betty Jo Teeter Dobbs, *The Janus Faces of Genius* (Cambridge University Press, 1991), 7.
27. Sotheby lot 31; Keynes collection MS 28. Also see René Buvet, "Le cas Newton," in *Bulletin du Grand Collège des Rites*, no. 117, 1992.

CHAPTER 4
THE BIRTH OF FREEMASONRY

1. *La fin des Corporations*, Fayard, 2001.
2. In *Le Monde des Lumières*, Fayard, 1999.
3. Oxford University Press, 1991.
4. George Allen and Unwin (London, 1981).
5. The Harvester Press, 1976.

6. "Les Lumières Maçonniques entre naturalisme et illuminisme," in *Renaissance Traditionnelle*, no. 130, 2002.
7. Thomas Sprat, *The History of the Royal Society of London, for the Improving of Natural Knowledge*, 2nd edition, 1702, 62–63.
8. J. T. Desaguliers, "The Newtonian System of the World, the best model of Government," 1728.
9. Pierre Boutin, *Jean-Théophile Desaguliers: Huguenot, philosophe et juriste*, 10.
10. Ibid., 12.
11. "The Royal Society and Early Grand Lodge Freemasonry," in *AQC* 80, 1967.
12. Pierre Boutin, *Jean-Théophile Desaguliers*, 134–136.
13. Bernard Jones, "La Grand Loge dite des anciens," in *Travaux de la Loge Nationale de Recherches Villard de Honnecourt*, no. 8.
14. In *Bulletin du Grand Collège des Rites*, no. 120.
15. Margaret C. Jacob, "Maçonnerie."
16. *Renaissance Traditionnelle*, nos. 113, 114, and 117.
17. Denoël and Gallimard, 1984 and 1999.

AFTERWORD

1. *Naissances mystiques* (Paris, 1959), 11.
2. Paul Hazard, *The European Mind*, tr. Jay Lewis May (Cleveland: World Publishing Company, 1963).

BIBLIOGRAPHY

Bibliography compiled by Irène Mainguy, librarian-archivist of the Grand Orient of France, and Alain Bauer.

Allan, Tony. *Isaac Newton*. Heinemann Library, Chicago, 2001.

Atkinson, Dwight. *Scientific Discourse in Sociohistorical Context: The Philosophical Transactions of the Royal Society of London, 1675–1975*. Lawrence Erlbaum, 1999.

Bauer, Alain. *De la régularité maçonnique*. Edimaf, 1999.

———. *Grand O*. Denoël, 2001, and Gallimard "Folio," 2002.

———, with Édouard Boeglin. *Le Grand Orient de France*. Que sais-je? PUF, 2002.

Besuchet, Jean-Claude. *Précis historique de l'Ordre de la franc-maçonnerie depuis son introduction en France jusqu'en 1829*, with biographies of the most famous members of the order. Paris: Rapelly, 1829, 2 vols.

Blamont, Jacques. *Le chiffre et le songe, une histoire politique de la découverte*. Odile Jacob, 1993.

Bord, Gustave. *La franc-maçonnerie en France des origines à 1815: Les ouvriers de l'idée révolutionnaire (1688–1771)*. Slatkine, 1985.

Boutin, Pierre. *Jean-Théophile Désaguliers: Huguenot, philosophe et juriste*. Paris: Honoré Champion, 1999.

Boydell and Brewer. *The Diary of John Evelyn*. Woodbridge, 1995.

———. *Particular Friends: The Correspondence of Samuel Pepys and John Evelyn*. Woodbridge, 1997.

Brewster, David. *Memoirs of the Life, Writings and Discoveries of Sir Isaac Newton*. Edinburgh: Thomas Constable and Co., 1855.

Brodsky, Michel L. *La Grande Loge Unie d'Angleterre*. Edimaf, 1999.

Cahiers de l'Herne. *Les textes fondateurs de la franc-maçonnerie*. 1992.

Chevallier, Pierre. *Histoire de la franc-maçonnerie française*. Fayard, 1984.

———. *Les ducs sous l'acacia ou les premiers pas de la franc-maçonnerie française 1725–1743*. Slatkine, 1994.

———. *Histoire de la franc-maçonnerie française*. Fayard, 1974.

———. *La première profanation du Temple maçonnique ou Louis XV et la fraternité*. Librairie philosophique, 1968.

———. *Le Sceptre, la Crosse et l'Équerre*. Honoré Champion, 1996.

Christianson, Gale. *Isaac Newton and the Scientific Revolution*. Oxford University Press, 1996.

Cohen, I. Bernard. *The Newtonian Revolution*. Cambridge University Press, 1980.

Coleridge, Samuel Taylor. *Les Sermons Laïques*. NRF Gallimard, 2002.

Compilation (under the direction of E. Saunier). *Encyclopédie de la Franc-Maçonnerie*. Livre de Poche, 2000.

Compilation. *Protestantism et FM*. IDERM colloquium, 1998; Edimaf, 2000.

Compilation. *Freemasonry on Both Sides of the Atlantic*. Columbia University Press, 2002.

Compilation. *Le parfait maçon*. University of Saint-Étienne, 1994.

Compilation. *La mort de Newton*. Maissonneuve et Larose, 1996.

Compilation. *Éléments d'histoire des sciences*. Larousse, 1997.

Combes, André. *Les trois siècles de la Franc-maçonnerie française*. Edimaf, 1998.

———. *Le Grand Orient de France au XIX*[e] *siècle*. 2 vols. Éditions du Rocher, 1998 and 1999.

Conduitt, John. "Memoirs of Sir Isaac Newton," in *Collections for the History of the Town and Soke of Grantham*. W. Bulmer and Co., Cleveland Row, 1806.

Corneloup, Joannis. *Universalisme et franc-maçonnerie: Hier et aujourd'hui*. Vitiano, 1963.

Coutura, Joël. "Essai pour un état administratif du G.O. au 1er janvier 1789," in *Bulletin intérieur de la commission d'histoire du GODF*, no. 8, December 1973.

Dachez, Roger. *Des Maçons opératifs aux Franc-Maçons spéculatifs*. Edimaf, 2001.

Daruty, Jean-Émile. *Recherches sur le Rite Écossais Ancien Accepté*. Télètes, 2002.

De Lussy, Florence. "Un peu de lumière sur les origines anglaises de la Franc-Maçonnerie." *Revue de la Bibliothèque Nationale* 12 (1984).

Désaguliers, René. *Les pierres de la Franc-Maçonnerie*. Dervy, 1995.

Dobbs, Betty Jo Teeter. *The Foundations of Newton's Alchemy*. Cambridge University Press, 1975.

———. *The Janus Faces of Genius*. Cambridge University Press, 1991.

Doré, André. *Vérités et légendes de l'histoire maçonnique*. Edimaf, 1991.

Étienne, Bruno. *Une Voie pour l'Occident, la franc-maçonnerie à venir*. Dervy, 2000.

Favre, François. *Documents maçonniques*. Librairie maçonnique, A. Teissier, 1866.

Ferrone, Vincenzo, and Daniel Roche. *Le Monde des Lumières*. Fayard, 1999.

Feuillette, Romulus. *Précis de l'histoire du Grand Orient de France*. Gloton, 1928.

Gilbert, Adrian. *The New Jerusalem*. Bantam Press, London, 2002.

Gould, Robert Freke. *Histoire abrégée de la franc-maçonnerie*. Guy Trédaniel, 1989.

———. *History and Antiquities of Freemasonry*. 3rd edition, revised, in 4 vols. Caxton, London, 1951.

Groussier, Arthur. *Constitution du Grand Orient de France par la Grande Loge Nationale*. Gloton, 1938.

Hall, A. Rupert. *Isaac Newton, Adventurer in Thought*. Oxford: Blackwell, 1992.

———. *Henry Moone and the Scientific Revolution*. Cambridge University Press, 1990.

Hall, Marie. *Promoting Experimental Learning, Experiment and the Royal Society, 1660–1727*. Cambridge University Press, 1991.

Hamill, John. *The Craft: A History of English Freemasonry*. Leighton Buzzard, Crucible, 1986.

Hawking, Stephen. *Commencement du Temps et fin de la physique*. Flammarion, 1992.

Jacob, Margaret C. *The Radical Enlightenment*. George Allen and Unwin, London, 1981.

———. *Living the Enlightenment*. Oxford University Press, 1991.

———. *The Newtonians and the English Revolution*. The Harvester Press, 1976.

Jouaust, A. G. *Histoire du Grand Orient de France*. Télètes, 1989.

Kaplan, Steven L. *La fin des Corporations*. Fayard, 2001.

Kervella, André. *La Maçonnerie Écossaise dans la France de l'Ancien Regime*. Rocher, 1999.

———. *La Passion Écossaise*. Dervy, 2002.

Knight, Christopher, and Robert Lomas. *The Hiram Key*. Gloucester: Fair Winds Press, 2001.

Knoop, Douglas, G. P. Jones, and Douglas Hamer. *The Early Masonic Catechisms*. Manchester, 1943, and new editions, 1963 and 1975.

———. *The Medieval Mason*. Manchester, 1967.

Koyré, Alexandre. *Études Newtoniennes*. NRF Gallimard, 1968.

———. *Du monde clos à univers infini*. Johns Hopkins Press, 1957, PUF, 1962, and Tel Gallimard, 1973.

Lamarque, Pierre. "Grand Orient de France et Grand Loge de Clermont au XVIIIe siècle," in *Bulletin intérieur de la Commission d'histoire du GODF*, no. 9, March 1974.

Lantoine, Albert. *Histoire de la Franc-maçonnerie française: La Franc-maçonnerie chez elle*, 3 vols. Nourry, 1925.

La Tierce. *Les constitutions d'Anderson*. Paris, 1742, and reprint Romillat, 1993 and 2002.

Le Bihan, Alain. *Francs-maçons et ateliers parisiens de la Grand Loge de France au XVIIIe siècle (1760–1795)*. Bibliothèque Nationale, 1973.

———. *Francs-maçons parisiens du Grand Orient de France (fin du XVIIIe siècle)*. Bibliothèque Nationale, 1966.

———. *Loges et Chapitres de la Grand Loge et du Grand Orient de France (deuxième moitié du XVIIIe siècle)*. Bibliothèque Nationale, 1967.

Lepage, Marius. *L'Ordre et les Obédiences*. Dervy, 1956, reprint 1993.

"L'histoire," special issue, *Les francs-maçons*, July–August 2001.

Ligou, Daniel. *Histoire des Francs-maçons en France*. Private, 1981.

———. "L'opposition du Grand Orient de France à l'introduction du Rite écossais Rectifié, 1775–1789," in *Renaissance Traditionnelle*, no. 11, July 1972.

———. "Notules sur l'histoire de la Franc-maçonnerie du Grand Orient de France, de 1789 à 1848," in *Humanisme*, nos. 97–98, July–October 1973.

———. "Pages d'histoire," in *Humanisme*, no. 99, January 1974.

Lomas, Robert. *The Invisible College*. London: Headline Books, 2002.

Luquet, Georges. "Grand Loge d'Angleterre et Grand Orient de France," in *Grand Collège des Rites*, supplement to the *Bulletin des ateliers supérieurs*, no. 37 (1952).

Lyons, H. *The Royal Society 1660–1940*. Cambridge University Press, 1944.

Mackenzie, Kenneth. *The Royal Masonic Cyclopedia*. Aquarian Press, 1877 (reprint 1987).

Mainguy, Irène. *La symbolique maçonnique du troisième millénaire*. Dervy, 2001 (3rd edition, 2003).

Manuel, Frank. *A Portrait of Isaac Newton*. Belknap Press, 1968.

———. *The Religion of Isaac Newton*. Clarendon Press, 1974.

Marcos, Ludovic. *Histoire du rite française au XVIIIe siècle*. Edimaf, 2000.

Marcy, Henri-Félix. *Essai sur l'origine de la franc-maçonnerie et l'histoire du Grand Orient de France*. Edimaf, 1986.

Martin, Gaston. *Manuel d'histoire de la franc-maçonnerie française 1721–1929*. PUF, Paris, 1934.

Maury, Jean-Pierre. *Newton et la mécanique céleste*. Découvertes Gallimard, 1990.

Miles, Rogers B. *Science, Religion, and Belief: The Clerical Virtuosi of the Royal Society of London, 1663–1687*. New York: Peter Lang.

Mourges, Jean. *La Franc-maçonnerie, société initiatique des temps modernes*. Dervy, 2002.

———. *La pensée maçonnique, une sagesse pour l'Occident*. PUF, 1988 (5th edition, 1999).

Muray, Philippe. *Les XIXe siècle à travers les âges*. Denoël, 1984, and Tel Gallimard, 1999.

Naudon, Paul. *Les origines religieuses et corporatives de la Franc-Maçonnerie*. Dervy, 1984.

Newton, Isaac. *Observations upon the Prophecies of Daniel, and the Apocalypse of Saint John*. Darby and Brown, 1783, reprint: Oregon Institute for Science and Medicine, 1991 and 2000, and his complete works.

Porset, Charles. *Les premiers pas de la franc-maçonnerie en France au XVIIIe siècle*. Edimaf, 2000.

Pouille, Armand. *Des Maçons médiévaux aux compagnons d'aujourd'hui*. Grancher, 2002.

Purver, Margery. *The Royal Society*. London: Routledge, 1967.

Quilliet, Bernard. *La tradition humaniste*. Fayard, 2002.

Ragon, Jean-Marie. *Orthodoxie Maçonnique, suivie de la maçonnerie occulte et l'initiation hermétique*. Dentu, August 1853.

Ramsay, Andrew M. *Principes philosophiques de la religion naturelle et révélée*. Glasgow, 1748, reprinted by Honoré Champion, 2002.

———. *The Travels of Cyrus*, 4th edition. London: James Bettenham, 1730.

Rebold, Emmanuel. *Histoire des trois grandes loges de Francs-maçons: Le Grand Orient, le Suprême Conseil, la Grande Loge nationale*. Collignon, 1864.

Revauger, Cécile. *La querelle des anciens et des modernes: Le premier siècle de la franc-maçonnerie anglaise*. Edimaf, 1999.

Rossi, Paolo. "Hermeticism, Rationality and the Scientific Revolution," in *Reason, Experiment and Mysticism in the Scientific Revolution*. New York: Science History Publications, 1975.

Schwartz, Hillel. *The French Prophets*. University of California Press, 1980.

Seife, Charles. *Zéro: La biographie d'une idée dangereuse*. J.-C. Lattès, 2002.

Sprat, Thomas. *The History of the Royal Society of London, for the Improving of Natural Knowledge*, 2nd edition. 1702.

Stevenson, David. *The First Freemasons: Scotland's Early Lodges and Their Members*. Aberdeen University Press, 1988.

———. *The Origins of Freemasonry: Scotland's Century, 1590–1710*. Cambridge University Press, 1988.

Stukeley, William. *Memoirs of Sir Isaac Newton's Life*. London: A. Hasting White, 1936.

Teder. *L'irrégularité du G.O.D.F. (origines réelles de la Franc-maçonnerie)*. Beaudelot, 1909.

Thory, Claude-Antoine. *Histoire de la fondation du Grand Orient de France*. Jeanne Laffitte, 1981.

Van Kley, Dale. *The Religious Origins of the French Revolution: From Calvin to the Civil Constitution, 1560–1791*. Yale University Press, 1996, and Seuil, 2002.

Verlet, Loup. *La Malle de Newton*. NRF Gallimard, 1993.

Vidal-Fezandie. *Essai historique sur la Franche-maçonnerie depuis son origine jusqu'à nos jours*. Lawalle-Neveu, Bordeaux, 1830.

Westfall, Richard. *Newton*. Cambridge University Press, 1980 and 1993; French tr., Flammarion, 1994.

White, Michael. *Isaac Newton: The Last Sorcerer*. Perseus Books, 1997.

Yarker, John. *The Arcane School*. Belfast: William Tait, 1909.

Yates, Frances. *The Art of Memory*. Routledge, 1966.

———. *Giordano Bruno and the Hermetic Tradition*. London: Routledge, 1961. French tr.: Dervy, 1988.

———. *The Occult Philosophy in the Elizabethan Age*. London: Routledge, 1979, and Classics, 2001.

———. *The Rosicrucian Enlightenment*. London: Paladin, 1975.

INDEX

Books of Related Interest

THE MAGUS OF FREEMASONRY
The Mysterious Life of Elias Ashmole—
Scientist, Alchemist, and Founder of the Royal Society
by Tobias Churton

GNOSTIC PHILOSOPHY
From Ancient Persia to Modern Times
by Tobias Churton

MOZART THE FREEMASON
The Masonic Influence on His Musical Genius
by Jacques Henry

THE SECRET HISTORY OF FREEMASONRY
Its Origins and Connection to the Knights Templar
by Paul Naudon

THE MYSTERY TRADITIONS
Secret Symbols and Sacred Art
by James Wasserman

SCIENCE AND THE AKASHIC FIELD
An Integral Theory of Everything
by Ervin Laszlo

SACRED NUMBER AND
THE ORIGINS OF CIVILIZATION
The Unfolding of History through the Mystery of Number
by Richard Heath

THE RETURN OF SACRED ARCHITECTURE
The Golden Ratio and the End of Modernism
by Herbert Bangs, M.Arch.

Inner Traditions • Bear & Company
P.O. Box 388
Rochester, VT 05767
1-800-246-8648
www.InnerTraditions.com

Or contact your local bookseller